THE ORIGIN OF MANCHU RULE IN CHINA

Frontier and Bureaucracy as Interacting Forces
in the Chinese Empire

THE ORIGIN OF MANCHU
RULE IN CHINA

Frontier and Bureaucracy as Interacting
Forces in the Chinese Empire

BY

FRANZ MICHAEL

1972

OCTAGON BOOKS
New York

Reprinted 1965
by special arrangement with The Johns Hopkins Press
Second Octagon printing 1972

OCTAGON BOOKS
A Division of Farrar, Straus & Giroux, Inc.
19 Union Square West
New York, N. Y. 10003

Library of Congress Catalog Card Number: 65-25880

ISBN 0-374-95605-7

Printed in U.S.A. by
NOBLE OFFSET PRINTERS, INC.
NEW YORK 3, N. Y.

To
OWEN LATTIMORE

PREFACE

This study of the Origin of Manchu Rule in China deals
with a period of Chinese frontier history. The Inner Asian
Frontiers of China—the mutual interrelationship of developments on both sides of the frontier—have been shown in a
new light by Owen Lattimore's studies and writings. In
this book I have tried to study this interrelationship through
a most significant period. I have attempted to analyze it
further; to show the importance of political organizations
and institutions, of their growth and development, for the
great processes formed by interacting forces in China's
history. To study these forces rathen than to give an exhaustive description of the period has been my aim.

I have to be grateful for much friendly assistance. It is impossible to state here all that I owe to Owen Lattimore. He
has been a teacher and a friend, never-failing in his advice,
criticism and encouragement.

Dr. Karl August Wittfogel has had the great kindness
to read the whole manuscript and to give me a number of
most valuable suggestions and criticisms. He has furthermore allowed me to read and make use of the manuscripts
of his own books on Liao history and on *Oriental Society
in Asia and Ancient America*, both soon to be published. I
wish to thank also Dr. A. W. Hummel for his kind permission to read various Manchu biographies from his biographical dictionary: *Eminent Chinese of the Ch'ing Dynasty*
which he is preparing. My colleagues at The Johns Hopkins
University have been most friendly in their advice. To Dr.
Sidney Painter especially who has taken it upon himself
to read and edit the text I am very grateful. Mr. David Lattimore has kindly read the proof.

This book was written while I was a fellow of the Walter

Hines Page School of International Relations at The Johns
Hopkins University. The acquisition by the School of the
private library of the late Erich Hauer, noted German scholar
in the field of Far Eastern Affairs, has greatly facilitated
my work.

FRANZ MICHAEL.

Baltimore, Md.,
   September, 1941.

CONTENTS

CHAPTER I

INTRODUCTION

At the end of the 16th and during the first half of the 17th century the northeast frontier region of the Chinese empire was the scene of a most important political development. A frontier tribe, later known as the Manchus, succeeded in building up in a comparatively short time a state organization which eventually became strong enough to conquer China. In 1644 a Manchu emperor ascended the dragon throne in Peking, and China fell under the sway of the Manchu dynasty, which was to rule until the revolution of 1911 ended the imperial history of China altogether.

The fact that a comparatively small tribe on the edge of China should succeed in dominating Chinese history for almost 300 years cannot be explained simply by military achievements. A military power not based on an elaborate social entity could perhaps be a destructive but not a positive and constructive factor. Indeed the "barbarian" conquests of China were not such simple affairs as imagination sometimes has pictured them. We are inclined to think of these "wild horsemen" from the Mongol steppes or from the forests and mountain valleys of Manchuria as something like an irrisistable force of nature sweeping over the plains of northern China. The descriptions of their conquests deal mostly with the wars they fought, the battles they won, the towns they took before their triumphant entry into Chinese capitals. Little is usually said about the real process of getting hold of the country.

So intensive an agricultural society as the Chinese could, however, not be conquered by riding over the land. If the outside invaders attempted more than a pure looting raid, if they were to remain in China, not only to conquer but to rule it, to attract enough Chinese groups to open the way thereto, they had to possess more than a "barbarian" organization.

1

This truth was once told to the greatest nomad conqueror of all times by a wise and upright captured official. When Ghenghis Khan had destroyed in North China the Chin dynasty, his men had taken captive one Yeh-lü Ch'u-ts'ai, who had served under the defeated dynasty. Yeh-lü Ch'u-ts'ai was a descendant of the "barbarian" dynastic family of the Khitan (Liao). As an official of the likewise barbarian Chin dynasty he had been trained and had served under the Chinese form of administration. His whole life experience had thus been with barbarian groups which had never given up their tribal traditions, but which had had to adapt their control of their Chinese agricultural subjects to the Chinese way. This man more than anybody else would understand the necessity for any barbarian conqueror to use Chinese forms of administration in agricultural China. "You have conquered the empire in the saddle, you cannot govern it so," was this man's advice to the Khan of all Khans.[1] And it was he who in the Mongol service was instrumental in creating the administration which allowed the Mongols later to subjugate and rule all China.

The importance of the gradual formation of these administrative organizations, of the intermediate stages, has not received great attention in histories of China. Owen Lattimore was the first to point out that the successful barbarian invaders of China did not come straight from the open steppes or the depths of the Manchurian forests. Looting raids were sometimes a first form of attack, but for the real conquest and domination an organization was needed that made of the horsemen, or added to them, administrators versed in the control of agricultural country and rural labour.

Such an organization could not be improvised. It had to be built up and developed slowly before a serious attempt to gain rulership over China could be made. Nor could it be created under entirely different social conditions outside of Chinese society. The most important political aspect of

[1] 天下雖得之馬上, 不可以馬上治, see Léon Wieger, *Textes Historiques*, Vol. 2, pp. 1657 f.

these invasions was therefore an organization starting at the margin of the Chinese world and proceeding simultaneously with further penetration into China and organization of " tribal " auxiliaries in the trans-Great Wall " hinterland." The foreign dynasties which set themselves up in China, as the Liao, the Chin, the Mongols and the Manchus, had developed a mixed culture on the margin of the Chinese society and thus " grew " into China, before they overran her. Only thus were they able to gain control and domination of the country.

This is very different from the so-called " assimilation " of invaders in China. The theory of " assimilation " would indicate that the " barbarians " came in as children of nature and then were made Chinese. There is some truth in the fact that physically the different kind of life, the greater luxuries and a good deal of laziness changed the people of the invading group within a few generations. But politically the word " assimilation " is misleading. It was not a change after the conquest of China. The change was necessary before the conquest was even possible. Only by becoming " Chinese " in their political organization had the " barbarians " a chance of conquering the rule over China.

A political organization of this kind, however, could never be solely an accumulation of offices and institutions. The group undertaking this task needed political thought, ideologies, a conception of the state. Not only the institutions and manifestations of Chinese political life had to be accepted by the rulers to be; but also something of the Chinese beliefs had to prepare the conqueror's mind for his new role. Chinese philosophy and organization were thus reaching out to the border and preparing there forces for a penetration and conquest of China.

All this meant a process of development that would take time. The conquest of China was not a military question alone, it was not even in the first place a military question. It was a question of the growth of a political organization, a process of amalgamation.

The Manchu conquest of China was not only the last but

also the most important and longest lasting [2] of the frontier invasions into China. This conquest followed the pattern described above of a slowly growing political organization suitable for the rule over Chinese society. This organization was built up while the Manchus penetrated that part of Manchuria which had been since ancient times Chinese and agricultural. It was another case of learning Chinese administration on a small scale before subjugating China.

*   *   *

The phenomenon of invasions and conquests of China by so-called barbarians was of course only a part of the whole political mechanism of the Chinese world. And the Manchus in their penetration from the frontier into China made use of circumstances which could be found at recurrent intervals in Chinese history. In order to be able to discuss the complex state organization of the Manchus, we must therefore first, shortly at least, outline the background of the Chinese political system, in which the Manchus were to play a part.

The most outstanding characteristic of Chinese history is the chain of dynasties succeeding each other in a line, usually interrupted by years of strife and chaos. Out of the recurrent chaos of rebellion there arose always a new dynasty which, after a time, reestablished the former order. The political system as such was never much altered. The dynasties passed through the stages of a cycle which started with the consolidation of newly gained power and led with more or less regularity over a time of highest success into decline and fall.

Conservative Confucian political theory explained this change of dynasties in a static Chinese world by the "will of heaven." The Chinese agrarian society gave the state only the task of upholding peace and order. This was the responsibility of the emperor, the bearer of a "heavenly

---

[2] The life of the Manchu dynasty was at the end artificially prolonged by the intervention of the Western Powers, without which the Manchus would probably have fallen during the Taiping rebellion some fifty years earlier.

mandate." As long as the emperor possessed "virtue," he retained this heavenly mandate. But when flood, drought or disorder showed that this virtue had disappeared, he would loose the mandate. The people could then revolt, overthrow the dynasty and put on the throne another dynasty which would hold the heavenly mandate in its turn.

Foreign scholars, sceptical of the will of heaven, saw the reasons for dynastic decay chiefly in the corruption at court, the eunuch system and the degeneration of the imperial family.

A number of modern scholars have sought and found a further, deeper functional explanation to this periodical change of dynasties which was always accompanied by similar circumstances. The first modern analysis of this cyclical system was fomulated by K. A. Wittfogel [3] and taken up by others. A rich and complete analysis of these dynastical cycles can be found in Owen Lattimore's recent book: *The Inner Asian frontiers of China*.[4] We will try to give here a very short, necessarily oversimplified, restatement of the mechanism of cyclical dynastic change in China.

The explanation is found in the Chinese system itself. The Chinese agrarian society was controlled financially and politically by the landed gentry, the class from which the state drew its officials. The landed gentry and the officials, being of one and the same social class, the "scholar gentry," worked the agrarian taxation system at the same time for the government and their private interests. The two interests were of course of a conflicting nature. And the first weakening of central control would allow the private in-

[3] See K. A. Wittfogel's article "The Foundations and Stages of Chinese Economic History," p. 53. The idea was taken up by Wang Yü-chüan in his article "The Rise of Land Tax and the Fall of Dynasties in Chinese History." See also K. A. Wittfogel's description of the cycles in "Die Theorie der Orientalischen Gesellschaft," pp. 109-114. The fullest picture of the economic circle in oriental society in general and Chinese society in particular is given in Wittfogel's new book, *Oriental Society in Asia and Ancient America*, to be published this winter by the Oxford University Press. Through Dr. Wittfogel's kindness the author has been able to see various parts of his manuscript in advance.

[4] Owen Lattimore, *Inner Asian Frontiers of China*, Ch. XVII.

terests to win out. The officials, aside from other possibilities of exploitation, could exempt their own property from taxation. The increasing burden on the property of the rest led to indebtedness. Since the great landholding families which supplied the official bureaucracy also engaged privately in money lending, exorbitant rates of interest would speed up the development that brought more and more property into the private hands of men who held official positions and thereby also exempted it from taxation. The government finances naturally would suffer.[5] The central control would be further weakened. This situation, combined with the accumulation of great private fortunes, the neglect of public enterprises such as irrigation and flood control, resulting famines, the unrest among the suffering and exploited farmers, became the basis of rebellion of the discontented people. If the rebellious movement became menacing enough, it would find the support of parts of the leading class, anxious to protect their fortunes. When this happened in important economic or strategic areas, the rebellious group would have a good chance to succeed.[6] A new regime would be started by the victorious leaders with concessions to the farmer. A stronger, stricter control over officials would be exercised at the outset. But the system would not be changed and the ruling class would remain the same. Thus the game could start all over again.

From the point of view of this cyclical system the most interesting period is the time of the decline of one dynasty, when new forces, bandit leaders, political figures with little to lose and much to gain had a chance to build up a new government. This is also the time for successful invasions. K. A. Wittfogel in his *Probleme der chinesischen Wirtschaftsgeschichte*[7] has pointed out that the conquest of China, always tempting for the surrounding barbarians, was

    [5] Wang An-shih's attempts at reform give a very illustrative view of his fight against such a development in the Sung time. See Williamson, *Wang An Shih.*

    [6] See Chi Ch'ao-ting, *Key Economic Areas in Chinese History.*

    [7] See K. A. Wittfogel, *Probleme der Chinesischen Wirtschaftsgeschichte,* p. 325.

naturally easiest at the time of political decay, of inner strife in China. Aside from the rumbling of Chinese inner revolts, which potentially would lead to new Chinese dynasties, there was also at such periods the possibility of outside conquest. Chinese rebellion and outside invasion became competitors for the prize of the dragon throne. Which of the two was in each case in a better position to succeed, depended on the political configuration at the time.

*   *   *

If one compares the development of outside barbarian groups with that of rebellious Chinese groups in this competition for control of China, one finds that they were by no means as different as one might be inclined to think at first. Both grew in a similar way, had to build up similar types of organizations and establish themselves at first each in certain definite regions, where they gained the base for further expansion, attack and final control of the country. The barbarians brought, of course, certain elements and political conceptions of their own with them. But, as already indicated, they had to adapt themselves to a Chinese form of political organization, had to use Chinese political instruments and, to a high degree, Chinese officials. They had to rule China in the Chinese way.

This fact has been somewhat obscured by the events of the recent history in China. The impact of the West has brought new factors into the political and social life of China. The arrival of Western merchants, industries, railways, gunboats and ideas upset and changed the usual course of events. China could with these forces be ruled in a different way. The security and unchangeableness of the Chinese system under whatever rule came to an end. To rule China meant no longer to have the benefits of agricultural taxation and live on it in the country. China, opened by force, became a "market" and later a possible reservoir of raw material and cheap labour. It could be controlled with the help of modern means of communication first from treaty ports and, as attempted to-day, even from outside the country. If China wanted to survive as an independent society it had to defend itself against this new and different menace. That could only be done by changing the Chinese society, adapting it to modern conditions, creating something which China had not been before: a national state. That meant not only a change of government. It meant a revolution.

China had not known a revolution in this sense since the beginning of its imperial history. There had been rebellions and revolts, civil war, invasion and conquest, but the system always remained the same. The ruling group changed, but not their political ideology, nor their method of government, nor the scholar-gentry class necessary for this type of government. Now, however, a change of system became necessary and a national union had to be formed of the Chinese society. With the revolution of 1911 a first attempt was made in this direction. It remained partial and was altogether not very successful. But it destroyed the old form and started a transformation which has since gone further.

With the necessity of transformation there came also the necessity of a new ideology. As the conditions of the new world for China had been created by the West, it was also Western thought that influenced and started the Chinese revolution. Western ideas of democracy and nationalism were used as propaganda by the revolutionists in their struggle against the Manchu dynasty. This influence was rather sudden and without sound preparation. It was propagated in China by men, some of whom came from the new merchant class of the treaty ports, though others were modern representatives of the old scholar-gentry. Still others like Sun Yat-sen represented the millions of Chinese who had gone abroad as coolie laborers and petty merchants during the second half of the nineteenth century, where a few of them acquired great wealth—notably in Malaya. Some of these new Chinese political theorists were rather superficial in their "Westernism." Others were rather superficial in their "Chineseness"; for while discrimination against the Chinese living abroad kept them loyal to China, the environments in which they lived were un-Chinese. Thus the theorists' knowledge of Western things remained often rather limited and was not always well digested, while their knowledge of Chinese tradition was sometimes not very profound. We find that certain modern, outspokenly foreign and hitherto non-Chinese ideas were not only applied to the time of the revolution, but that Chinese history became reinterpreted in the light of such new thought. In his *San Min Chu I*, Sun Yat-sen accuses the Manchus of having destroyed Chinese "nationalism" by introducing "cosmopolitanism." The revolutionists called the Manchus "alien intruders" and serious Chinese writers on political science have used many arguments to prove that the Manchus were not "rightful successors" to the Ming throne,[8] but only "conquerors" and therefore China had to be freed from them.[9]

All these ideas were of course modern and did not fit into the old Chinese world, the world of the time of these "barbarian" and "alien" invasions. Confucian state philosophy did not know the national state. It did not differentiate between nationalities or races. "When the barbarian enters China (i.e. Chinese civilization) he becomes Chinese" (夷而進於中國則中國之) states a Confucian saying. Besides, the majority of the "Manchus" at the very time when they moved into China were racially of Chinese stock, as we shall later see. They did not aim at anything else than at what the Chinese rebels of the same and other periods had aimed at, namely to establish a "Chinese" dynasty. That they used force and conquest was also not unusual. True, the emperor who held the heavenly mandate and followed the kingly way, was according to the orthodox interpretation supposed to have gained his position by his virtue rather than by the force of arms. But Chinese political reality could never do without force. No Chinese dynasty, from outside or inside the country, ever gained the throne without recourse to arms. In this way there was no

[8] As the Manchus themselves had claimed at the time for reasons of political propaganda.
[9] See Hsieh Pao-chao, *The government of China* (1644-1911).

essential difference between conquest from outside and from inside the country. Of course, like other invaders, the Manchus kept a part of their own traditions together with their adaptation of Chinese ways. We shall have to study this development of their organization. But as a general system they had to accept the Chinese way of life and Chinese civilization.[10]

If we study the organization formed by the Manchus before they seized power, we must then be careful not to bring in thoughts and conceptions of another time. It is the working of the cyclical and competitive forces in Chinese history, as described above that will interest us here.

*   *   *

From this view point the period with which we have to deal is of particular interest. The Ming dynasty was in decline. Peasant unrest and revolts created armies of bandits starting out from Shantung and from Shansi and ravaging the countryside in China. The rebellion swept to the capital and for a time it seemed as if a new Chinese dynasty might be established by its leader.

In the meantime the Manchus organized their frontier state. When finally the Mings fell and the dragon throne was in their reach, the Manchus were ready to grasp for it.

Both rebellion and invasion had then a fairly equal chance of success. The scale was tipped in favour of the Manchus by the weight of several factors. They possessed a better organization and leadership. The Manchu success was only possible because of the base the Manchus had built in their

[10] The ideological fight between the Chinese revolutionists of 1911 and the Manchu dynasty was therefore not so much a struggle between Chinese and alien conquerors, as it was a clash between the forerunners of a modern Chinese national state and the representatives of the old Chinese Confucian tradition. It has even been said that the Manchu dynasty " was more Chinese-Confucian than any previous dynasty had been. Every member of the ruling family had a profounder Chinese education than the leaders of the revolutionary party, except of course the group of K'ang Yu-wei." See Haenisch, " Die gegenwärtigen chinesischen Wirren und ihre geschichtlichen Voraussetzungen." This statement has to be modified, however, by the realisation that even with their education the Manchus—as we shall see—never became quite absorbed into the Chinese life.

state formed at the edge of China. But, most important of all, the Manchu policy was, as we shall see, more " Chinese " than that of the Chinese rebel who was the Manchus' rival! So well had the Manchus come to understand and to apply the Chinese system of government that the country turned to them rather than to an unorthodox Chinese.

We shall try to analyse this development. In studying the genesis of the Manchu rule in China we shall show this transformation of a frontier force into a dynasty of the Chinese empire. We shall discover that this was not a simple one-line development. The Manchu acceptance of Chinese bureaucracy had been preceded and facilitated by a certain feudalization of the frontier regions. A dual process from within and without the Chinese agrarian frontier created a sphere of transition through which the Manchus could pass into China. Outward and inward forces opened thus in their interaction the way for a new dynasty.

This creative dual process was not limited to the Manchu period. It was a characteristic part of Chinese history. The case of the Manchus seems however particularly suited to demonstrate this development.

CHAPTER II

MANCHURIA AND ITS PEOPLES

The region where the Manchus founded their political organization was especially suited for the development of a frontier state through the interaction of bureaucratic, feudal, tribal or clan elements. It was by nature a region of contrasts where geographical conditions favoured different forms of human society and economy side by side—a frontier par excellence. This region's present name: Manchuria, is of Western origin and without equivalent in the Chinese language and is historically misleading. It seems to indicate a uniform country with a uniform people. This Manchuria was not.

The name Manchuria came into use only in connection with the conflicting interests of the Great Powers over a region in which the way of life in modern times has changed entirely, chiefly through the modern means of railway communications. Today Manchuria, although called by the Japanese "Manchukuo," has an overwhelming Chinese population which has spread rapidly along the railways over a great part of the arable land.

In past history, however, Manchuria was not a country with either definite borders or a uniform people, but rather an area of contact of different types of life and societies. There was the Chinese society, agricultural in its economy and bureaucratically administrated. There were the steppe nomads and stock breeders and the forest people, living in tribal or feudal organizations.

In recorded history the oldest and most mature part of Manchuria was the extreme south, southwest and southeast, which was old Chinese cultural ground. The lower plains of the Liao river, the narrow strip of plain along the coast line on the northwest of the gulf of Liaotung down to Shanhaikuan, the shores of the Liaotung peninsula and

12

the lower valley of the Yalu river lent themselves to an intensive irrigational agrarian economy comparable to that of North China. In this region there lived from neolithic times people with the same characteristics and the same mode of life as those in North China.[1] Their history was a part of Chinese history. Together with the rest of China they had advanced from early feudalism to the Chinese bureaucratic form of government of the imperial age.

Yet, though Chinese in its way of life, this region was geographically rather isolated from the rest of China, separated from it by mountains, steppes or the sea. For normal constant communication in terms of trade, taxes in kind, " barbarian " tribute missions passing through on the way to the capital, the coming and going of officials and other people there was but one narrow land route to be followed. That was the narrow strip of agricultural land between the gulf of Liaotung on one side and the mountains of what is to-day Jehol on the other. The narrowest point was the strategic pass of Shanhaikuan, where the Great Wall comes down to the sea and one enters China Proper. This road connected Chinese Manchuria with the rest of China. Other routes, further inland, leading from China through the mountain passes, steppes and grassland of Jehol into Manchuria were not practical for normal communications. The lack of cultivation along these routes made traveling or transportation of goods too difficult and expensive. These routes were good for mobile raiding parties and armies and were thus used by barbarian invaders. The Manchus themselves after their conquest of Chinese Manchuria made looting campaigns into North China over these passes. Until they had undisputed control of Shanhaikuan, they were, however, not sure of permanent access to China Proper over these Jehol routes alone.[2] All the more important appeared thus the precarious route through Shanhaikuan.

[1] Owen Lattimore, *Inner Asian Frontiers of China,* pp. 103 ff.

[2] Without the passage through Shankaikuan they could not keep connection with the conquered towns in Hopei and lost them again. See *K'ai Kuo Fang Lüeh,* Ch. XIII, p. 9. In this the Manchus differed from the earlier

The other important connection between Chinese Manchuria and China Proper was the sea route, in particular over
the comparatively short distance from the Shantung to the
Liaotung peninsula. This sea route created an interrelationship that showed itself in the origins of the Liaotung
people and their political connections. While in the Western
part of Chinese Manchuria many people had family links
with Hopei province, in Liaotung a great many Shantung
Chinese were to be found.[3]

With only one practical land route and otherwise sea
connections with China Proper the Chinese part of Manchuria was but an outpost of Chinese society and life. It
was vulnerable to attack and had therefore a particular frontier character.

Outside this Chinese basin and bordering on it were,
broadly speaking, two other types of peoples, societies and
economies in Manchuria. To the West and Northwest, in
the mountains and plains of Jehol and the Hsingan range
and beyond, the country consisted largely of rich grassland
and open steppes. The steppe society populating these regions in varying strength and political combinations was related to that of other parts of Inner and Outer Mongolia.
It was a nomad society of tribal peoples of Mongol or related origin. Their economy was based on the herding of
horses, sheep, cattle or camels on the pastures of the steppe.[4]
They lived in tents and their strength lay in the mobility
of their tribal groups.

Khitan and Juchen, peoples of Manchuria which formed the Liao dynasty
and the Chin dynasty which flourished in the eleventh and twelfe centuries.
(For a short valuation of their organizations see below.) Each of these
dynasties occupied and was partly based on the mountains and grass lands
of South and North Jehol, which regions at that time had some sedentary
population. They thus had direct access to the Peking-Tientsin plain and
were not dependent on the narrow Shanhaikuan passage. When the Manchus
were rising to power, however, Jehol was occupied by Mongol tribes, not
yet under full Manchu political control.

[3] Many of the Chinese in Manchuria who went over later to the Manchus
originated either from Hopei or Shantung. The rest were born in Manchuria, but the families had often Shantung or Hopei connections.

[4] For the difference " between the stockbreeders of Jehol and the steppe
nomads of Mongolia " see Wittfogel-Feng, *Liao*, section 1. (Compare note
9 below.)

There was, however, no fixed natural frontier between the last arable acre and the steppe. A gradual transition and diminuition of returns created a marginal zone of changing economy.[5] This zone would serve to allow a changing steppe group to grow into China, or for Chinese groups to break loose into the steppe, according to the political strength and configuration on the inside and outside.

This kind of interrelationship between the Chinese kind of society and that of the steppe and grassland Mongols existed in Manchuria as well as in other regions of the Mongolian border with China. In Manchuria we find the same mixed frontier groups as elsewhere along the marginal zone. The control of these zones would at times serve the Chinese to extend their domination far into the steppe.[6] At other times it would serve Mongols as stepping stones to gain control over Chinese Manchuria or China Proper. In between such periods there would sometimes develop in the marginal zone little hybrid states, feudal in their political organization, with walled towns and a mixture of agriculture and pastoral economy.

The Mongol groups of the steppes were, however, not the only frontier problem of the Chinese basin in Manchuria. To the north, northeast and east, in the forests and marshes along the Hurka, Sungari, Ussuri and Amur rivers and in the valleys of the Chang-pai-shan or Long White Mountains lived a variety of tribes of Tungus origin. They were primarily hunting and fishing nomads, yet differed among themselves considerably in their life and use of animals and equipment. In the north the reindeer was used, in the east we find dogsleds and canoes. But the main part of these tribes that came into contact with the Chinese world used— probably at first under steppe influence—horses. Their chief domesticated animal was the pig. Its major economic importance was reflected in the religious rites of the shaman-

[5] Owen Lattimore, *Inner Asian Frontiers of China*, pp. 480 ff.

[6] The beginning of the Ming dynasty was a period in which Chinese control extended far into Jehol. Compare T. C. Lin, "Manchuria in the Ming Empire." This fact can be explained by the marginal, partly sedentary, economy created in Jehol by the Liao and their Mongol successors.

istic tribes. They had also a certain amount of desultory agriculture. And we can even believe that this type of agriculture was "original" with them and not at first accepted from the Chinese. The Manchus, themselves one of these Tungus tribes, had in their own language a good number of words for agricultural products and implements.[7]

Like the steppe nomads these hunting nomads had intermittently been in contact with the Chinese basin of Manchuria. The mode of life and the political organization in the adjoining regions had consequently been considerably affected. Again as with the Mongols, intermediate small feudal states with a type of settled life, with a greater emphasis on agriculture, with strongholds and walled towns would originate and lead to political transformations. At times these little states would be under the political control of the Chinese. At other times, when Chinese frontier control became lax, one of them could become the starting point for a strong frontier power which in its turn would penetrate the Chinese basin in Manchuria or beyond it into China Proper.

The three different types of societies and peoples, the Chinese, the Mongols and the Tungus were in no way static towards each other. The whole of Manchurian history is a constant movement, a melting and a new separation of these elements. The traces of these contacts and transformations had, of course, been left in the characteristics, tradition and even racial stocks of the groups concerned. Groups from the steppe and the forests that had penetrated the Chinese basin and became settled there, remained after their political control was ended. Others left again, but took with them the knowledge of Chinese life and, most likely, Chinese adherents and slaves too. And sometimes Chinese that had penetrated the barbarian regions became " barbarian " themselves.[8]

[7] F. Otte, " Early Manchu Economy," gives a list of such words handed to him by E. Hauer.

[8] Thus we find among the Manchus clan names that indicate Chinese origin. Of one of the clans, Irgen Kioro, we know that it consisted of the

Out of all these elements states were formed. In the course of years they fell apart again. Some remained just little frontier states, others became the cradles of Chinese dynasties.

The economic basis for all political development was, however, always the Chinese agricultural, sedentary society. Any barbarian dynasty to be set up had to gain its economic power through the rich return in taxes from the Chinese parts of its frontier state. Sometimes North China—Hopei, Shansi (and Shensi) provinces of our time—would be the Chinese agricultural base of such frontier states. The Liao government for example, based upon the pastoral centres of Northern Jehol, gained its chief revenue and subsistence economy from these North Chinese regions.[9] But, leaving Jehol aside, for Manchuria and Manchurian political development it was the Chinese agricultural heart of the country, as described above that would serve as base fore economic political power.

Whoever held control over this agricultural center with its rich income was politically ascendant over the outlying regions. The agricultural basin of Manchuria within the range of soil and water that favoured the Chinese way of life was thus the key to any political organization of Manchuria. Its economy and settled society formed the dominating influence under whatever rule it lived. It could be conquered. But when the surrounding tribes wanted to penetrate the Chinese basin, they had to adapt their organization first to the Chinese form of economic life in order to

descendants of Sung princes who had been originally brought there as prisoners. See L. Gibert, *Dictionnaire Historique et Géographique de la Manchurie*, p. 357.

[9] The history of the Liao and their complicated system of half tribal and half bureaucratic administration has now been fully revealed with richest material in the volume *Liao* by Karl August Wittfogel and Feng Chia-sheng, the first to appear soon in the series *History of Chinese Society* brought out by the Chinese History Project at Columbia University under the direction of Dr. Wittfogel. Through Dr. Wittfogel's kindness the author has had the privilege of using the Liao manuscript before its publication. The economy of the Liao is dealt with in section II; the political institutions are given in section XIV of the Liao volume.

profit from and to exploit the productive power of the region. That meant the necessity of bureaucratic administration of the Chinese type. The regions outside thus remained always under the shadow of Chinese Manchuria; even if it was a Chinese Manchuria under "barbarian" rule. Of the three regions of Manchuria, the Chinese agricultural part was thus the political and therefore also the cultural center.

Yet strategically there was a hitch in this superiority. When the Chinese were strong, they could make from this region successful invasions of steppe and forest—as they did in the early Ming time. But even then the Chinese could not occupy these outlying regions because the latter did not lend themselves to Chinese economy and social life. When on the other hand the Chinese organization in the agricultural basin was weakened, the wealth and decisive political importance of this heart of Manchuria became an immediate incitement for outside groups to attack the region and to form there new political organizations.[10] All that the Chinese could do against this possibility was to attempt to keep the outside groups apart and thus prevent them from getting strong and dangerous. The policy of *divide et impera* was applied. A sort of vassalage relationship with each single small group was established and they were played one against the other to guarantee the balance of forces, in itself the guiding principle of Chinese frontier policy. There was a constant danger in this policy and it could only be upheld as long as the Chinese organization, always somewhat isolated from the rest of China, was strong and intact.

This difficulty of guarding outlying regions that could not be occupied was not limited to the Chinese in control of this agricultural center. Interestingly enough a "barbarian" ruler, once established there, would meet the same difficulty with regard to other barbarians. Whoever held this agricultural region, Chinese or conquerors, had to be strong enough to defend it and keep the outlying regions under some form of "remote control." The political organization

[10] No natural barriers or obstacles protected the settled Chinese region from such attacks. But palisade walls were several times erected as defense.

to cope with this problem would in each case be similar. The Chinese basin would have under Chinese or "barbarian" control a bureaucratic administration. The outlying regions would in each case be kept separated under feudal regimes.

Yet there was a difference in the "center of gravity" between Chinese rule that extended into the outlying regions and "barbarian" domination that had taken root in Chinese territory. In the latter case the "barbarian," though drawing his strength from the Chinese basin, had his origin in some part of the outlying regions. This home part, although feudal or tribal, would keep a predominant influence in the common organization. The dualism of bureaucratic and feudal form of government would thus be a greater problem with a barbarian group on Chinese soil than with a Chinese government. We have here a problem for which the Manchus, as we shall later see, found a more harmonious solution than former "barbarian" dynasties.

The history of Manchuria gives many examples of the combinations of these three Manchurian societies. Since ancient times a number of local states or kingdoms based on the settled agrarian life of a greater or smaller part of the Chinese basin had been formed by peoples from the outlying regions. The region of modern Hsinking, which was the focal point of the three different societies, and northwestern Korea were especially suited as main bases for such smaller states. The Huimai, the Kaokoli, the Muoho and the Pohai were examples of such kingdoms.[11]

In between, the Chinese regained their hold over Manchuria. The periods of the Han, the Sui and the Tang dynasties were the times of strongest Chinese control. But after the 10th century not only Manchuria, but at first northern and finally all China came under the domination of "barbarian" dynasties for almost half a millenium.

Two of these barbarian dynasties originated in Manchuria. The Liao came from the partly forested mountain valleys

[11] A comprehensive outline of Manchurian history is found in Gibert, op. cit., pp. 51 ff. and 591 ff.

and plains of Jehol with their rich grazing grounds. The Chin came from the eastern rivers and mountainous forest regions of Manchuria. Both conquered Chinese territory and established their economic power-center there; the Chin in Chinese Manchuria, the Liao mainly in North China. The development of their power naturally shows interesting parallels to the later Manchu rising.

The Liao dynasty (907-1125),[12] formed by the Khitan, a group of Mongol tribes in Jehol, established their state in Jehol, Chinese Manchuria and parts of North China and expanded from there chiefly into the Northwestern regions. They not only subjected agricultural regions in North China and Manchuria, but settled a great number of farmers, particularly from Manchuria, on patches of land in their own region of Jehol. They strengthened thus the marginal character of this region which remained the strategical center of power.[13]

The Liao used Chinese officials and introduced Chinese administration.[14] But the administration of their own pastoral tribal world and of the subjected agricultural regions and populations remained strictly separated. Their whole territory was divided into five circuits with five different capitals. Within these circuits the Chinese world[15] had a bureaucratic system of town administration, prefectures and

[12] These dates have been chosen following Wittfogel's determination. The year 907 was the time of the establishment of the hereditary dynasty. The penetration into Chinese territory and the adoption of the dynastical name of Liao came later.

[13] See Wittfogel-Feng, *Liao,* section I.

[14] See Wittfogel-Feng, *Liao,* section VIII. Compare also *Liao History,* Ch. I and 74, p. 2a, with regard to the Liao's Chinese adviser Han Yen-hui, who played a part under the Liao similar to that of Yeh-lü Ch'u-ts'ai under the Mongols. He " founded towns, markets, fixed the border of the land, allowed settlement to the people who had been Chinese subjects. He regulated the relationship between husband and wife, taught agriculture and procured food for the people. Therefore it became rare for anyone to flee or rebel. If the emperor T'ai-tsu could firmly establish his rulership, build towns and palaces, establish law courts, arrange the relationship between emperor and officials (*sic!*), take the title T'ai-tsu, stipulate laws and customs, it was Han Yen-hui, who had made all this possible." (Quoted from Gabelentz translation of Liao history, pp. 9-11.)

[15] Including the P'o Hai of Manchuria.

counties, while the Khitan were governed under their own pastoral tribal system. A few feudal organized groups and frontier towns with military bureaucracy played a minor part.[16] It was a completely dualistic system, a politically and economically "amphibian empire," as Wittfogel calls it.

This dualism created many difficulties. It kept the two parts of the state separated, mutually distrusting each other, with the various subject people always ready to throw off the yoke when occasion arose. The surviving tribal institutions and kinship cohesion were responsible for violent inner struggles all through the Liao period. These bloody inner fights were largely caused by succession questions and competition for the throne, due to the violation of the traditional tribal rules of succession. And this fighting weakened the strength of the Liao dynasty considerably.[17]

On the other hand the Liao, based on Chinese soil, encountered in their relationship towards the outlying regions the same kind of difficulties which a Chinese dynasty would have had. At the height of their rule their power ranged far to the northwest and north into Outer Mongolia and toward Turkestan. During this period it was revealed that a tribe of frontier origin which had acquired Chinese agricultural possessions, was subject to the same handicaps in frontier control as a Chinese dynasty. The wider its prestige in the steppe, the sooner the point of diminishing returns was reached in the control of frontier tribes.[18] The same was true for the Liao control of the Tungus frontier in Eastern Manchuria. Some unruly Tungus frontier people were settled in the "civilized" agricultural way under a native "governor." They were of the Ju-chen tribe and 150 years later themselves organized a powerful frontier com-

[16] "The Ch'i Tan were governed according to their national system, while the Chinese were governed according to their own system. The national system was simple and crude. In the Chinese system the usage of the traditional terminology was preserved." *Liao History*, Ch. 45, pp. 1 a-b, quoted from Wittfogel-Feng, *Liao*, section XIV, which describes in detail the political organization of the Liao.

[17] Wittfogel-Feng, *Liao*, section XIII.

[18] See *Liao History*, Gabelentz transl., pp. 120-2; Wittfogel-Feng, *Liao*, section XIII.

bination, penetrated further into the Chinese world, defeated the Liao in a prolonged struggle and inherited their power and imperial position. Their victorious prince founded the Chin dynasty (1115-1234).

The Chin rose thus on the " tribal " frontier of the Liao, when the Liao state with its dualistic tribal-military control over Chinese revenues developed a China-like vulnerability to predatory tribalism.[19]

The Chin had a development similar to that of the Liao before them. Their administration of the Chinese agricultural region of Manchuria followed the pattern of their Mongol predecessors. They ruled Manchuria and North-China from five different capitals under a quasi-Chinese system of administration, while their people and army remained tribal-feudal as had those of the Liao. But with their settlement in China and Chinese Manchuria they also became subject to the difficulties of frontier control when their power was weakened.

The Liao had come from the steppe frontier of Manchuria, the Chin from the forest frontier. Now the pendulum was to swing back to the steppe frontier again. In the steppe domain of Mongolia a rivalry between Turks in the west and Mongols in the east led to ascendancy of the Mongols under their famous ruler Genghis Khan. He and his successors defeated in several stages the Hsia kingdom in Northwest China, the Chin Empire and the Sung Empire in South China until Genghis' grandson Kubilai established in China the Yüan dynasty (1280-1368). These Mongols (now in the narrow sense of the word) had not originated in Manchuria.[20] Their state was organized elsewhere. Manchuria had to be conquered only to cover their flank and exterminate the Chin there. This fact explains that for Manchuria the

[19] The Chin were cousins to the later Manchus. The story of the early submission of neighbouring tribes, the flight of one rival into the camp of the Liao where he found support, etc., give a number of interesting parallels with the later Manchu history.

[20] Ancestors of Genghis Khan had, however, been minor frontier employees of the Chin.

rule of the Mongols meant "une période de décadence."[21] The country became badly depopulated with the exception of the steppes of Jehol. The majority of the administrative centers of the Chin was suppressed, because they were not needed when the Mongols established their capital at Peking.

The administration, however, remained bureaucratic. Agricultural Manchuria became a province with seven districts or Routes, Lu (路), and the Capital in Liaoyang. But besides his civil administration the Mongol Yüan dynasty placed military units with feudal hereditary commanders and officers in all Lu.[22]

All three barbarian dynasties, the Liao, the Chin and the Mongol Yüan had thus administered the Chinese basin of Manchuria and conquered China under the Chinese form of civil bureaucratic administration. Their own military might was kept apart in feudal or tribal form. It was a dualistic form of political control! Tribal-feudalism and bureaucracy remained side by side in their government. Only the Manchus succeeded later in merging these two inherent factors of the Chinese world state and thus created a government that was a more complete and longer lasting fusion of frontier and Inner China than had been accomplished by any former frontier government in China.

For this task the Manchus could profit from past experiences and developments. The Manchus originated from a Tungus border tribe, the Ju-chen.[23] They were thus related to the founders of the Chin dynasty who had lived 300 years earlier. Their background was certainly not the original hunter and fisher society of the Manchurian forests. They were not only good horsemen, but their military suc-

---

[21] Gibert, op. cit., p. 45.

[22] The so-called Wan Hu Fu (萬戶府). This was undoubtedly the same as the Mongol Tumen. Like the Chinese Wan, this means 10,000, but also multitude and was the major unit of Mongol military feudalism. These Wan Hu Fu were divided into upper, middle and lower for resp. 7000, 5000 and 3000 men. Their chiefs and other officers (Chen Fu 撓鎮) were hereditary. Compare Tze Yuan, Shen 51; see Hauer, K'ai Kuo Fang Lüeh, p. 617, note 52.

[23] Or Nu-chen.

cesses, like those of the Chin, owed much to their skill in mounted archery, an art that must have been developed by the steppe nomads. From the Chinese part of Manchuria these Ju-chen tribes had accepted a greatly extended agriculture and a life in walled towns. They maintained a flourishing border trade with the Chinese. And when their time came, the Manchu knew the historical lesson—that any strong frontier state had to be based on the agrarian center of Manchuria. Their task was then to blend their own organization with that of the Chinese state, attach the Mongols to it and thus form a unit of the three peoples of Manchuria. In this endeavor they found a new farther reaching solution of the frontier problem of the dual forces of feudalism and bureaucracy. It was the preceding Chinese Ming dynasty that had paved the way to this solution.

CHAPTER III

THE MING ORGANIZATION IN MANCHURIA

The history of both Chinese and barbarian dynasties based on Manchuria or ruling Manchuria indicates that control of the region as a whole always had a dual requirement: Administration and the main sources of revenue had to be based on the " Chinese basin "; but strategy always required a special military cadre of a separate and peculiar frontier character. These two requirements could never be coordinated in an entirely stable, integrated state structure. There was always a little extra weight on either the military requirement or the requirement of revenue and bureaucratic administration. This emphasis was bound, in the course of time, either to increase or to shift in the opposite direction. Either process led to conflict between the loosely coordinated but unintegrated and heterogeneous elements of the composite state. And when this conflict went far enough it led to the rise of a new dynasty, attempting to cope afresh with the old problems.

This did, of course, not only hold true for Manchuria. The problem was similar at other points of the Chinese inland frontier. Control over the regions of the frontier and beyond was a political and military necessity for China. These regions formed therefore an inevitable element in the conception of the Chinese Empire and in its system of government.

The Chinese Empire consisted really of two parts. Its center was the Chinese agricultural society. The administration of this center had become increasingly bureaucratic ever since Tsin Shih Huang Ti destroyed the feudal confederation of old and created the empire. Chinese society had by then outgrown the regional limitations under which a feudal system could work efficiently. The tasks of the government in irrigation, defense and other administration had become too general. The feudal lords had already ad-

25

vanced from the use of labour to taxes in kind, and now the bureaucratic state was ruled on a kind and money basis.[1]

Yet not the whole Chinese world had become bureaucratic. We have seen that the Chinese political influence extended beyond the confines of the Chinese agrarian society. This was necessary as a measure of protection if nothing else. But the people of the frontier and outside of it could not, in the tribal or feudal condition of their societies, be ruled in a bureaucratic way. This part of the Chinese Empire had to be controlled on a feudal basis.

Political philosophy, formed in accordance with actual conditions had to make allowance for this dualism. And Chinese political philosophy allowed, indeed, a very vast and general interpretation. Confucianism, the official state philosophy of the Chinese empire, was bureaucratic on the whole. Confucius, teaching during a period of dying feudalism and coming himself from obscure aristocracy, had aimed at an antifeudal bureaucracy, regardless of rank.[2] But while the aristocracy of old was destroyed and all power transferred to the emperor, China did not become an organized national state in our sense of the word. The emperor was really the constitutional expression, and indeed the only one [3] of a common culture. The Chinese empire was a great unity of civilization. From the Chinese view point theirs was the only possible civilization, which was far superior to any barbarian life outside. Yet this unity had to include barbarian regions. It was therefore all-embracing, and in its conception a world state. The people outside would share

[1] See Wittfogel, " Foundations and Stages of Chinese Economic History," pp. 40-51.

[2] The idea of Confucius as the prophet and creator of a non-feudal ideology with ethical training and qualifications of the new official in contrast to the military feudal virtues of old has been formulated by Wittfogel in his " Foundations and Stages of Chinese Economic History," pp. 49/50. The concept of Confucius as the creator of the philosophy " of the bureaucratic way of life in its most civil, most literate and most cultured form " is given more fully in Dr. Wittfogel's forthcoming book: *Oriental Society in Asia and Ancient America.*

[3] " L'empire n'a d'autre fondement que la vertu propre à une dynastie. Hors de l'empereur l'Etat n'est rien." Granet, *La Civilisation Chinoise*, p. 158.

in a " benevolent " way as far as possible in the benefits of this civilization. The emperor, entrusted with the heavenly mandate, was the son of heaven and the responsible mediator between heaven and the people on earth. These were then not only the Chinese, but also the neighboring nations through the medium of their rulers. The relationship between the Chinese emperor and the rulers of the neighboring states or small tribes was regarded as a vassal relationship, a feudal suzerainity.

The Chinese empire consisted thus constitutionally of two spheres. The regions with Chinese agricultural society, China in the narrow sense of the word, were administered bureaucratically under officials directly responsible to the emperor. The outer spheres were connected in a vassal relationship with the head of the Chinese civilization. At the frontier, as in Manchuria, these two different constitutional elements were in constant contact. We have already seen how they interacted in reality and still remained separated, dualistic, an unsolved problem.

It was this problem that the Chinese Ming dynasty (1368-1644) tried to solve in a new way. What the first Ming rulers had in mind was in particular a strengthening of the local defense of the agrarian regions against outside attacks. We have said before that these attacks were always possible when the weakening of central control would invite the frontier people to gain control of North China or the rich Chinese basin of Manchuria. We have described the weakening process itself as being caused by the officials of the scholar-gentry class, working for their own benefit rather than for the central government. The weaker the emperor's power became, the greater was the independence of the local gentry through its local wealth and influence in regional affairs. In theory the emperor was still omnipotent. But in practice the life of the local communities, or rather of the local ruling groups, became more and more autonomous.

The chief disadvantage of this tendency towards localization in Chinese political life was the fact that it was a localization of privileges more than of responsibilities. The central power was weakened by the enrichment of the local gentry, but not relieved of its tasks by local assets.

This was especially true of the question of defense. Defense was traditionally the task of paid armies of riff-raff and a responsibility of the central government. A financial weakening of the central government naturally rendered more difficult the payment of large mercenary armies, although more needed in difficult times. The concentration of such armies largely in the capital made their upkeep particularly expensive. The scholar-gentry on the other hand owed its monopoly of administrative posts to its educational monopoly. For it the army, representing the central power signified an unwished-for supervisory pressure, against which "moral sanctions" were sought. Brutal force in contrast to the frailty of the scholar was stigmatized. And the soldier's profession became despised to the utmost by the leading class.[4] For the scholar-gentry there was more security in the administrative monopoly of their class, always needed, under whatever rule, than in the force of arms.

This unequal contest between the imperial power and the local classegoism of the gentry made the securing of the agricultural frontier against outside attacks particularly difficult.

There had been, in Chinese history, interesting attempts to solve this problem. The most important of them had been undertaken in the Sung period (eleventh century) by the statesman and reformer Wang An-shih.[5] It was the time when the last Chinese dynasty for over a century to come struggled against an ever more threatening northern invader. Wang An-shih's plan was to develop a militia army. The advantages of his plan were numerous. Financially the militia was much cheaper to maintain and would, and did indeed, allow a very substantial decrease of the much

[4] For the old and new type of Chinese soldiers see Olga Lang, "The Good Iron of the New Chinese Army," *Pacific Affairs*, March 1939.

[5] Compare Williamson, Wang An Shih. Wang's other important reform attempts—the most serious attempts ever made to reform the Chinese political system—cannot be described here.

more costly standing army. Militarily the fighting value of
the militia, supported by the best elements of the region,
was far superior to the hired riff-raff of the standing army.
The militia was furthermore at the spot to uphold the peace
not only against foreign aggressors, but also against the local
banditry.[6]

The militia scheme—like Wang's other reforms—was
strongly opposed by the bureaucratic class, because a
"healthy" militia would have created a new quasi-feudal,
embryo elite of men whose appeal was to their armed followers, not to the classics. Wang An-shih's reforms were
thus undone by his conservative successors, and fifty years
later the Sung were driven from all of North China. Finally
the South too fell under the rule of the invading power.

A somewhat similar reform was now tried again by the
Ming dynasty. The Ming took up again the idea of a local
military organization and thus knowingly or unknowingly
followed the example of the great Sung statesman. The
bureaucratic civil administration, as it had been developed
by long tradition, was maintained by the Ming for China
Proper. The country was subdivided in provinces, prefectures
and districts. But in addition to this civil administration, or
rather beside it, a special military organization was set up.
The Ming created the so-called Wei (衛) or military
guards.[7]

These Wei were regional military establishments, located
at strategic places in between the civil administrated districts. They were most important along the sea coast to

[6] The danger of this system was the possible strengthening of local political
forces, which might become independent. This was one chief objection of
the time and is a consideration that has to be kept in mind with regard to the
later Ming organization in Manchuria.

[7] Compare *Ming Shih,* Chüan 27, Chih 52, Chih Kuan (職官) 15, p.
7257. The name "Wei" was in use before the Ming, for instance for the
Chinese translation of the ordo of the Khitan by the expression Kung Wei
(宮衛). The meaning is however in this case that of a tribal, not a bureaucratic, military institution. Yet, institutions similar to the Ming Wei were
not unknown in former Chinese history for border protection. But they had
been frontier posts, never organizations of whole agricultural regions. To
study their development might bring interesting results.

guard against invasions by Japanese pirates and on the Northwestern frontier. They were also found in strategic places inland, especially to protect the imperial canal.[8]

These Wei were in themselves a complete military administration, so that the Ming bureaucracy was in itself dualistic. The civilian districts had a greater share in taxation, the military districts supported and controlled the troops. The Wei, consisting of about 5600 men, were subdivided into larger and smaller So (所) or posts, of 1120 and 112 men respectively.[9] The So consisted of two general banners (旗總) of 50 or more men and ten small banners (小旗) of 10 or more men each. These guards and posts were under the direct command of regional high commanderies and these in turn under the orders of the military board of the five armies at the capital.[10] The army was hereditary and registered.[11] We have thus a complete separate military administration of a regional kind.

This was the Ming administration of China Proper. In Manchuria the Ming went further than this dualistic system of intermediate civil and military administration. While in other parts of China these Wei were established parallel with and between the civil administration, in Chinese Manchuria only military districts were formed.

As we have seen, Manchuria had been greatly depopulated under the Mongols. When the Ming defeated the Mongol dynasty, a Manchurian Mongol leader, Nahach'u, surrendered after some fighting. His followers and their families, probably a mixed Mongol-Chinese group, some 200,000 strong, were settled in Liaotung and Liaohsi (east and west of the Liao valley) in the Chinese basin of Manchuria,[12] thus making the Mongol element in the weakened Chinese

[8] Compare *Ming Shih*, Chüan 27, Chih 52, Shih Kuan 5, p. 7257.
[9] Compare Chapter II, note 11: the military organization of the Wan Hu Fu of the preceding Mongol Yüan dynasty.
[10] Compare T. C. Lin, " Manchuria in the Ming Empire," p. 26.
[11] Compare *Ming Shih*, army system: ping 2, p. 7293, Chüan 89, Chih 65. See also Tze yuan, shen 159, compare Hauer, *K'ai Kuo Fang Lüeh*, p. 618, note 53.
[12] See Gibert, *op. cit.*, p. 49.

basin particularly strong. The Chinese hold over Manchuria seemed therefore somewhat precarious. To strengthen it, the Ming organized the whole region of the Chinese basin into military guards or Wei exclusively.[13] No other administration existed within the region.[14]

In Liaotung, the Eastern part of the Chinese basin, 25 guards were stationed at strategic points; nine of them along the coast and the rest at communication centers. The High Commander was in Liaoyang. One guard at Tung-ning, consisting of five and later of seven posts, was formed of settled Ju-chen immigrants,[15] a fact that may have facilitated the later quick submission of this region to the Manchus.

For the Western part, Liaohsi, the High Commandery was at Peking. There were at first twenty guards and posts in this region; the greater part of them was however in marginal pastoral territory.[16] They were soon given up to the Mongols.[17]

From the strictly civil point of view Liaotung and Liaohsi were regarded as parts of Shantung and Hopei provinces for those branches of administration that could not possibly be executed under military administration. Thus the candidates from Liaotung and Liaohsi for the examinations of the civil service had to go to Shantung and Hopei respectively.[18]

[13] Another measure was the building of a palisade wall to defend the Chinese basin against outside attack. In this the Ming followed other precedents.

[14] A short attempt at civil administration in Liaotung was given up again in 1373 after two years. This was before Nahach'us defeat in 1375. See Lin, *op. cit.*, p. 26.

[15] Near Liaoyang.

[16] Lin, *op. cit.*, pp. 27/8, with a number of further references.

[17] Lin, *op. cit.*, pp. 30/1, speaks of the vital strategic importance of the loss of these guards in and along Jehol under the Ming. The real reason that they disappeared is most likely to be seen in the economic conditions of the region. Under various Mongol rules this region of Jehol had remained politically a center of power, and efforts had been made to settle agricultural sedentary population wherever feasible. Now, with impaired importance of the region, the marginal agriculture must have greatly suffered and the maintenance by the Chinese of bureaucratically administered sedentary military guards must have become impossible in the long run.

[18] Compare for the whole organization Meng Sen, *Ch'ing-Ch'ao Ch'ien Chi*, pp. 12-18.

If the administration of the Chinese basin had thus gained a regional and frontier aspect, life itself had also changed its forms somewhat. In contrast to the steppe society the Chinese agriculture would be expected to use all cultivable land for the plough. Yet we hear that great pasturages in Liaotung were set aside for horse raising. Under emperor Taitsu the Ming had a bureau for horse inspection, and a little later in 1406 a bureau for horse breeding was established. Six divisions were under its control, each in charge of four stud farms, which meant 24 stud farms for Liaotung alone. In its best time Liaotung had over 400,000 horses registered.[19] The Ming wanted thus to become selfsufficient in the horse supply needed for frontier fighting and defense. But the sound of galloping hoofs and the military discipline of the communities of the guards and posts created a frontier atmosphere with dangerous outlooks. The frontier would thus be protected against looting or organized attack. But once the center of power, the imperial government in Peking, became weakened or disorganized and the ties binding the regional administration to the center loosened, the danger that these parts would break off would be hightened. The whole of Chinese Manchuria had become frontier zone.

More than that. With their Wei the Ming had created a type of administration that would stand in good stead for any barbarian group that hoped to penetrate Chinese ground. Their problem had always been to fit their society to the Chinese bureaucratic government. With the Liao, the Chin and the Yuan this had led to a dualism of administration. This dualism helped to bring about the fall of these dynasties as their frontier-barbarian states were undermined by over-bureaucratization. Under the Ming now this dualism was for the frontier region alleviated by these military bureaucratic guards, assimilating the feudal frontier. This projection of bureaucracy proved later too great a burden for the bureaucratic Ming state to carry. But the bridging of the dualism by the Ming with their regional military

[19] T. C. Lin, "Manchurian trade and tribute in the Ming dynasty," pp. 866 f.

organization facilitated the breaking off of these parts from China and, most important, it showed the barbarians a way by which their society could more easily be blended with the necessary Chinese bureaucracy! Indeed, the " Wei " of the Ming became the prototype of the coming Manchu banner organization! Even the term " banner " had already been used by the Ming, although for smaller units than the later Manchu banners. In this sense the Ming prepared the way for the later barbarian Manchu group to " grow " into China.

This " preparation " was not limited to the Chinese basin of Manchuria. In their policy towards the outlying regions the Ming created likewise the conditions which facilitated later transformation.

We have said before that the bureaucratic Chinese conception of the state allowed, nevertheless, a sort of feudal vassal relationship between the Chinese emperor and the kings or chiefs of neighboring states or tribes. The extent of such control naturally varied greatly in practice in Chinese history.[20] In Manchuria the first half of the Ming period meant a genuinely far-reaching Chinese control over the outlying regions. This control was exercised by division of the regions into districts with the same names for posts and guards, So and Wei, as used in the administration of the Chinese agrarian basin of Manchuria and also—in between civil administration—in China Proper. But these native guards and posts were, except for the name, something very different from the Chinese military bureaucratic organization at home. They were the subdivisions used to keep the native groups apart and prevent them from combining to form a dangerous power. The old principle of divide et impera was clad in a new garment.

The native guards and posts were not really military in character. They were a device to advance and confirm the native chiefs in their position as local lords and rulers. Not

[20] The existence of " tribute " to the emperor, or " presents " to the vassal princes did sometimes cover a relationship of Chinese ransom to prevent attack or looting expeditions.

only could one group thus be kept from controlling others, but the tribes themselves could be broken up into smaller units, each independent of the others and directly responsible to the Ming High Commanderies. It is noteworthy that the Manchus later copied the same method and applied it in subdividing the Mongol tribes, especially in Inner Mongolia.

The tribes recognized already the hereditary succession of leadership. The Ming succeeded—and this again was later imitated by the Manchus—in making this succession dependent on their confirmation. And this confirmation was not automatic. It had to be deserved and was only given for one grade lower than that possessed by the predecessor in the official hierarchy. The same rank as the predecessor had to be gained by merit. The possibility of supporting rival candidates remained also a strong deterrent.[21]

Various ways existed to secure the loyalty of the chiefs of tribes or clans to the emperor and the Chinese local government. Aside from simple confirmation of their position, this position could be made more dignified by bestowing upon them titles and outer signs of recognition. There were all sorts of ranks, appellations and names, of robes, caps, belts and other awards, attractive not only for "uncivilized" people.

Most important, however, was the title to the geographical region combined with the position. It was the bestowing of what really amounted to a fief. For, a policy of keeping these units permanently apart involved not only hereditary leadership. To break up the dangerous mobility of the frontier tribes it was necessary to attach them to a definite territory, to its land, jealously guarded by their chiefs against encroachment from other tribes.

The easiest way to create an attachment to the land was to promote agriculture. Yet that was not everywhere equally feasible. It would naturally be more difficult therefore, to

---

[21] Sometimes such strife between relatives attempting to gain the same vacant lordship would lead to further subdivision of a unit. Thus the Chienchow guard, the cradle of the later Manchu state, was in the middle of the fifteenth century divided into two "wings" because of the rivalry of local chiefs. Later it became united again.

break the mobility of the tribes in the steppe and grasslands where agriculture was difficult. This may explain the fact that the Ming were not able to uphold for long the separate guards they had established in Jehol and the Mongol steppes of Manchuria.[22] But the attachment to a definite territory under local rulers was more easily accomplished over the Ju-chen world including the mixed Mongol-Tungus region to the North of Kaiyuan. We know that the Tungus forest tribes had from of old a certain amount of agriculture. The history of Manchuria with its movement of peoples to and from the Chinese basin had increased this knowledge of agricultural life. On this basis the Ming succeeded in creating a great number of what amounted to little feudal states or lordships. For a while the Ming controlled not only the frontier groups, but practically all of the Tungus region.[23] Naturally, the further one went from the center of Manchuria, the less one would find settlements with influence of Chinese agriculture and town dwelling. The original hunter and fisher type of life would survive; and the peoples' dependence on the Chinese administration could never have

[22] The Manchu succeeded better in dividing the different Mongol tribes into Leagues and Banners, alloting to each definite regions for summer and winter pastures with mounts marking the intertribal border lines. The Ming had established first a number of guards in southern Jehol which were originally under the High Commandery at Taning. In addition the Mongol tribe of the Urianghai-Kharchin further north was divided into three guards. But after their support had been needed by the emperor Cheng Tzu in his coup d'état, the region of Taning was given up to the Urianghai and the military or quasimilitary administration withdrawn. The control of the Ming over the Mongol tribes was from this time on precarious.

[23] Following the example of the Mongol Yüan dynasty the Ming reached out even to the mouth of the Amur where they established the High Commandery of Nurgan for the control of the Ju-chen people. At the height of their power the Ming had divided the Ju-chen world into over 200 guards, posts, stations and camps. This included not only the so-called Hai-hsi Ju-chen (海西) in the region around Harbin and the Sungari river, and the Chien-chow Ju-chen (建州) in the region of Ninguta, Sanhsing and the slopes of the Ch'ang-pai-shan, but also the so-called Wild Ju-chen in the regions of the Ussuri and lower Amur. Yet a sign of decay appearing at the moment when their power reached its peak could be seen in the fact that one of the Ming commissioners who established this system was a eunuch. See also Lin, " Manchuria in the Ming Empire," p. 29.

been for long much more than nominal.[24] But the Ju-chen on the frontier of the Chinese basin easily accepted the territorial idea. They developed a number of small states with walled towns, agriculture and hunting.[25] For them the old tribalism with its hereditary nobility plus the new agricultural settlement on the land led to feudalism. In this combination of tribalism plus territory their feudalism resembled that developed in Europe after the fall of the Roman empire.

It is this feudal world which was the first step toward Manchu political greatness. Tribalism, feudalism, regional bureaucracy, is the scale of its development. And the Ming had created in the Chinese basin as well as on the frontier the favorable conditions for their growth.

Not only in the political field had the conditions been favorable. To keep the frontier states peaceful and friendly the Ming had allowed them the possibility of profitable trade. The trade, as all trade under the Chinese form of social life, was controlled by the Chinese officials. It was strictly limited to definite markets at regular times at determined places. The trade was barter and, in the first line, official. After the official trade had taken the best parts, a controlled and taxed private trade was permitted. The development of such markets was a good indication of the development and importance of the different frontier states. And the Manchus got a good share of them.[26] These markets,

---

[24] " They lived east of Ninguta along the coast and on rocky islands and were cut off from the Ming frontier and far away. They were subject in name only and nothing more." *Sheng Wu Chi*, p. 3a, see Hauer, *K'ai Kuo Fang Lüeh*, p. 616, note 28.

[25] See *Sheng Wu Chi*, same page.

[26] At first trade was started at the Mongol side with the steppe people. The first and following markets were chiefly horse markets, serving simultaneously the Ming need for cavalry horses. While the Mongol Urianghai had three horse-markets, the Ju-chen people had at first only one market at K'ai-yuan. But when the Chien-chow Ju-chen moved down to the east frontier of the Chinese basin in the Ch'ang-pai-shan mountains, a special market was opened for them at Fu-shun. When they became stronger three more markets were opened for this Juchen group. See Lin, " Manchuria, Trade and Tribute in the Ming Dynasty," pp. 866 f.

in which silk, cloth, salt, etc., were exchanged for horses, cattle, furs, ginseng, etc., were "not only economic assets but also accelerated the impact of Chinese culture—a fact most significant in the development of the political ambition and capacity of this tribe." [27]

It is, however, important to note that except for a very few commodities—the cheaper kinds of cloth, salt—trade was not in consumer goods, but in luxuries. Not being an exchange of necessities it was all the easier to control politically, channelling the profit into the hands of chiefs. On the Chinese side, aside from the profits made by the officials, some individual merchant would often become wealthy, but the merchant class as such did not become politically powerful. [28]

Aside from these markets another kind of trade grew under cover of the feudal system described above, and the Ju-chen-Manchus had their share in it. Like other native princes and vassals of the Chinese emperor they were obliged to send tribute to the court in Peking. This tribute was for the sender something like a privilege, as these yearly tribute missions became quasi-trade missions. In exchange for the tribute, the bearers received ample presents; and they were furthermore allowed to take other goods along for barter or selling. The tribute was a small price to pay for the glamour and the luxury trade of the Chinese emperor and helped to strengthen the finanacial position of the Ju-chen leaders and their knowledge of things Chinese.

The political balance could not be forever upheld by this dividing and placating policy of the Ming. The frontier tribes, developing under Ming support an organized state life, would use the first occasion of Chinese weakening to organize greater political combinations. In this frontier atmosphere the nucleus was formed for the Manchu power

[27] See Lin, *op. cit.*, p. 870.
[28] This was the characteristic of all past trans-frontier trade. It never substantially influenced the Chinese economic system. There is therefore an enormous difference from the development of Western commodity and raw material (colonial) trade in the nineteenth century.

that was to gain the dragon throne of China. The Ming policy itself had created the condition from which the Manchus could profit for their necessary political transformation. The outgoing political tide of the Ming was followed by the incoming tide of the Manchus. We have so far discussed the background and conditions which enabled the framing of the Manchu organization. Now let us see the rise of the Manchu power and the building of their organization.

CHAPTER IV

THE RISE OF THE MANCHUS

We have described how the Ming dynasty attempted to render harmless the frontier tribes and to gain control over them. The Ming created for this purpose little feudal states to which they gave the same names of guards and posts, Wei and So, which they used for their own military regional units. One of these native feudal guards and frontier statelets, the Chienchou guard, became the cradle of the Manchu power. This guard was located on the east border of the Chinese basin in the Ch'ang-pai-shan, the Long White Mountains. Its capital town became Hsingking in the Ch'ang-pai-shan. At the end of the Ming period it had become one of a number of rival feudal frontier statelets.

The people that formed this small native state were a group of Ju-chen (Jurchid), a Tungus people already mentioned. To distinguish them from the Ju-chen tribes they were called the Chien-chou Ju-chen.[1] They were near relatives of the Ju-chen that had formed the Chin dynasty.[2] Under these names: as Chien-chou Ju-chen and soon making use of the traditional value of the name of Chin they

[1] The Chienchou Juchen group, as far as we can trace them back, had originated further north at Sanhsing, in the middle section of the Sungari river valley. They had migrated from there via the Hurka River and Ninguta to the Ch'ang-pai-shan and their location on the border of the Chinese basin, possibly reoccupying regions which their ancestors had held before them. Compare Owen Lattimore, *op. cit.*, pp. 117 ff. See also Chapter III, note 23.

[2] Owen Lattimore has pointed out that " Chienchou " may be a euphonic corruption from an original form Chintsu, " tribe of the Chin "; the fact that the name Chienchow was brought by this Juchen group down to the Ch'ang-pai-shan from its former homes on the Sungari corroborates this suggestion. See Owen Lattimore, *op. cit.*, p. 116, note 29. Owen Lattimore, *op. cit.*, (p. 115) describes the Manchu as deriving from " outlying tribal followers " of the Chin. Somewhat fantastic sounds Gorski's thesis that the founder of the Manchu power Nuerhaci was a direct descendant through ten generations from a prince of the house of Chin. See Gorski: " Ueber die Herkunft des Stammvaters der jetzt in China herrschenden Dynastie Zin und vom Ursprung des Namens der Mantschu."

39

started out on their historical career. Much later only, in 1635, shortly before their conquest of China did they adopt the new name "Manchu,"[3] to indicate for propaganda reasons that they had started a new page in history.[4]

The origin of the Manchus, then, was in a small frontier group, numerically at first unimportant, but holding a favorable political and trade position and formed by the Ming into a feudal administrative unit. Like others of these feudal units, the Manchu-Chien-chou guard was not static. A great deal of inner and outer conflict kept the political affairs of these feudal units in constant movement. They each consisted of several kinship groups. And the loyalty of the groups—and even within the groups—to lords and overlords depended on the latter's power to organize and to protect the group. Small feudal families could withdraw their allegiance from one lord who did not prove strong and form an independent group or join another combination.[5] The Chinese attempted to stabilize the frontier. Yet any weakening of Chinese supervision could lead to separation or junction of families and clans and the extension of power and territory of one ruling group.

That was the case when after initial expansion the Ming lost finally any direct rule over the outer regions and had to resign themselves to playing politics. The frontier states could raise their heads, could fight among each other for predominance, and a strong leader could attempt the formation of a larger state. The setting was ready for any powerful personality with political ambitions.

[3] The etymology of the name Manchu is still doubtful. Gorski, *op. cit.*, sees in it a Juchen word with the meaning "chief," "superior," "master" (in contrast to serf), that was later only extended to the whole people. Hauer (*K'ai Kuo Fang Lüeh*, annex, p. 592) explains it as derived from Manjusri, in this case the personal name (as often with Mongols and Tungus) of an ancestor of Nuerhaci, called by the Chinese Li Man-Chu. This name was then later used when a new name was sought for the group.

[4] Gibert, *op. cit.*, p. 54, note 1; Owen Lattimore, *op. cit.*, p. 116. See also biography of Nuerhaci in A. W. Hummel's coming biographical dictionary, *Eminent Chinese of the Ch'ing Period,* which the author has been kindly permitted to see in advance.

[5] The Chienchou guard had been part of the time divided into a left and right wing, each under its own feudal chief.

It is interesting to see how in this and parallel situations in Chinese history such leaders arose. Owen Lattimore has pointed out that as a rule these men started from very precarious and small beginnings.[6] A ruler in safe control of a given group would not lightly start a struggle for supreme power and thus endanger his present position with the possibility of losing everything he had. The man who had nothing to lose, who had to fight even to establish himself in a position inherited by feudal law from his ancestors but menaced by others might be swept and forced by his first victory into the road of fighting and struggle that would finally lead to a throne.[7]

Naturally, the candidate for such an ambitious policy had to have not only great natural gifts of leadership, but would also need personal experience of the forces he had to counter and to make use off. A feudal frontier leader in Manchuria, in order to be successful, had not only to be able to deal with the other feudal groups, but he had also to know the Chinese world enough to handle it.

In Nuerhaci, the founder of the Manchu state, such a leader arose. Nuerhaci (1559-1626), was first a feudal lord in the Chien-chou guard. He knew the Chinese world by personal experience as he had been to the market at Fushun,[8] and had personally gone on tribute missions to Peking.[9] He had played the part of a sort of interpreter and had thus known the Chinese " colonial service." He must thus have been acquainted with the Chinese political conceptions and their methods. And it was Nuerhaci personally who later against the advice and will of his feudal entourage

---

[6] Owen Lattimore, *op. cit.*, pp. 119, 540, 543.

[7] In the bureaucratic world the leaders of rebellions would similarly spring up mostly from the lower strata of the official class. Men who had failed in examinations, who had lost their job, been unfairly treated or even fugitives from justice would be potential leaders of rebellious bands. See K. A. Wittfogel, " Die Theorie der orient. Gesellschaft," p. 113, and Owen Lattimore, *Inner Asian Frontiers of China,"* pp. 72, 540, 543.

[8] See T. C. Lin, " Manchuria trade and tribute."

[9] In 1590 Nuerhaci led more than 100 junior Juchen tribal chiefs to carry tribute to Peking. Compare Nuerhaci's biography in A. W. Hummel's *Eminent Chinese of the Ch'ing Period.*

insisted in moving his capital into newly conquered Chinese centers, emphasizing frequently the importance of the Chinese basin, of land and people and agriculture.[10]

In the feudal world he was born. But he was one of the men, characterized above, that had to fight at the outset for their very existence. Called to leadership after his father's death, Nuerhaci had to assert himself at first in his own domain against dangerous rivalry. He had to start from unbelievably small beginnings to gain the inherited position of leader. We read how he carried on petty fights with the help of just a handful of followers; of nightly attempts on his life which he, alone in his house with his wife and children, had to avoid by ruse and bluff.[11]

His rival, a Manchu nobleman known as Nikan Wailan, had caused in a looting raid on another town the death of Nuerhaci's father and grandfather. This raid had been executed with Chinese support. In order not to lose all authority, Nuerhaci had to avenge these deaths and to fight Nikan Wailan. But the latter was protected by the Chinese who tried to play the two rivals against each other. When Nuerhaci became too presuming, they threatened to support Nikan Wailan as chief of the whole guard. In destroying his rival Nuerhaci had therefore to oppose the Chinese officials of the frontier. He had to carry on a struggle that lead to the inclusion of smaller neighboring groups under his domination, until he finally crushed his adversary, whom the Chinese by then no longer dared to support (1586).[12]

Not only the Chinese were concerned about Nuerhaci's growing power. His feudal neighbors became equally alarmed. The most important of these neighbors were four little states at the north of the Chinese basin known as the Hulun group. They were called Yehe, Hata, Hoifa and Ula. They stretched from the forest frontier to the region where steppe and forest met near the Chinese basin. At least Yehe,

[10] *K'ai Kuo Fang Lüeh*, Chapter VII.
[11] *K'ai Kuo Fang Lüeh*, Chapter I (1584).
[12] *Ibid.*

the westernmost of them, had a strong percentage of Mongol blood.

This Hulun group, located in the strategic region where all three Manchurian types of society touched, was naturally very important for the Chinese policy and consequently supported if menaced. These Hulun states had now become jealous of Nuerhaci's growing power. The former disunity of the neighboring Chien-chou state must have been to their liking. The new successful ruler of the Chien-chou group found in them distrusting opponents. These opponents obtained the support of the Chinese and Nuerhaci was forced into further fighting. That does not mean that a peace loving ruler was forced to war by his bellicose neighbors and that thus all the wars were caused by Nuerhaci's opponents. The change of the local balance of power could not be carried out without natural resistance of the threatened rulers. At first Nuerhaci was on the defensive, defeating a combined attack of the Hulun states against his own territory.[13] Then he himself started after 1599 a program of counter attack and conquest in which he finally destroyed both his feudal adversaries and the Chinese power protecting them.

A look on the map shows us how Nuerhaci was able to defeat one after the other the Hata, Hoifa and Ula states. To destroy the most distant state of this opposing Hulun group, it was necessary first to clear his flank from the Chinese who supported his adversary. Only after Nuerhaci had conquered the Ming town of Fushun in 1618, had destroyed in the following year the powerful Ming armies sent against him, had taken the northern Ming towns of Kaiyuan and T'iehling, was he able to destroy finally the last of his feudal rivals of the Hulun group, the Yehe state (1619).[14] It was a dramatic moment, when the last feudal rival, Gintaisi, the leading prince of Yehe sought death in the flames of his burning castle. Manchu legend tells of a curse he hurled down from the tower to his enemies before his death, threatening that the Manchus themselves would perish one

[13] *K'ai Kuo Fang Lüeh*, Chapter II.
[14] *K'ai Kuo Fang Lüeh*, Chapters V and VI.

day by a woman from Yehe and that thus his clan would be revenged.[15]

With this victory Nuerhaci had gained the uncontested rule over the feudal frontier. But it was no longer a feudal frontier fight which he was leading. The preceding penetration into Ming territory gave Nuerhaci's advance an entirely different character. Already, in 1616, Nuerhaci had proclaimed himself Khan or emperor. He had taken the device T'ien Ming (天命) and had called his dynasty Hou Chin or Late Chin, to indicate that he was to take up the imperial claim of his racial ancestors, the Chin.

This meant that he no longer regarded himself as fighting in defense of his position, but had started on an ambitious program. At first Nuerhaci had had no such imperial ambitions.[16] But with his eating grew his appetite.

The fighting had carried Nuerhaci far into the Chinese region. He followed up this advance and moved further. In 1621 the Ming towns Liaoyang and Shenyang (Mukden) were conquered and with this the whole eastern part of Chinese Manchuria or Liaotung fell into Nuerhaci's hands. Most towns surrendered and the remaining strongholds were captured.[17]

The comparative smoothness and easiness of this conquest of the whole eastern part of Chinese Manchuria in a short time indicates that transformations on the Chinese as well as on the Manchu side had prepared this transfer of power. Some of these transformations have been indicated already. Others will be discussed in more detail in the following chapters. Here the general strategy of the Manchu rise must be traced.

Nuerhaci took immediate advantage of his conquests. They were for him not temporary invasions. He transferred his capital to Liaoyang and later to Shenyang, indicating

---

[15] Because of this curse no women from Yehe were taken into the imperial harem. The only exception over 200 years later was Yehonala, the famous empress Tze-hsi, who was, because of her reactionary policy, regarded by many as the final cause of the downfall of the Manchus in 1911.

[16] K'ai Kou Fang Lüeh, Chapter I, sentence before last.

[17] K'ai Kuo Fang Lüeh, Chapters VII and VIII.

that he was to establish himself in the Chinese basin for good, and to found there a new kind of state. At the same time Nuerhaci secured his right flank by alliances with Mongol tribes starting with the Kalka and Korcin, submitting others by force. When he then attempted to conquer the rest of Chinese Manchuria, its western towns and regions, Nuerhaci met for the first time defeat at the hands of the Chinese governor Yuan Ch'ung-huan. The defeat was caused in part by technical superiority through the use of guns that had been made for the Chinese by Western missionaries. But it also may have been influenced by the fact that here the Chinese organization was still more intact, while the Manchu transformation had not yet gone far enough to appeal to traitors in this region. Nuerhaci, himself wounded in the fighting and depressed over the failure of his further plans, died in 1626. His imperial temple-name is T'ai-tsu.

His ninth son and successor Abahai, imperial temple-name T'ai-tsung, carried on his father's plans. He tried to negotiate a peace with the Chinese governor Yuan, who had defeated his father. No agreement was reached, but the negotiations prevented Ming interference while Abahai attacked and subjugated Korea, securing thus his left flank. It is probable that the negotiations were only delaying tactics on Abahais' side. In any case immediately after the subjugation of Korea, he attacked Yuan again, but was again repulsed (1627). Frustrated in his frontal attack, Abahai or T'ai-tsung as we shall call him, extended further his alliances and campaigns in the Mongol world. From there he invaded North China in 1629/30 through the mountain passes of Jehol, avoiding the Chinese held towns of Eastern Manchuria and the pass at Shanhaikuan. But without this connecting link, the invasion could not lead to any lasting conquest, and the towns conquered in North China were quickly lost again. The campaign had one important result— the Manchus got rid of their strongest opponent, governor Yuan, who was falsely accused of treason at the court in Peking and imprisoned.

The coming years brought a slow conquest of the remaining Chinese parts of Manchuria with a simultaneous increase of Chinese troops and officials in the Manchu ranks and further transformation of the Manchu government. The hold over Mongol tribes was extended and another transitory backdoor invasion of China Proper, this time through Shansi, took place in 1632.

In 1635 T'ai-tsung called his people Manchu and his dynasty Ta Ch'ing to destroy all traces of former submission to China.[18] Tai-tsung now openly became a contender for the rule over China. In a new campaign Korea was forced to recognize this position, become a vassal and discontinue all relations with the Chinese Ming dynasty.

To strengthen their own racial group in the growing political structure, the Manchus undertook frequent raids and missions into the Tungus hinterland to fill their ranks with people brought from there by force or persuasion. From 1636 to 1644 the whole Amur region came under their control.

In 1639 another backdoor invasion of China Proper took place. And in the coming years the remaining towns of Chinese Eastern Manchuria fell one after the other. It was, however, not given to T'ai-tsung to live to see himself in Peking. He died in 1643. Only one year later inner disorder brought the collapse of the Ming and gave the Manchu regent Dorgon the chance to complete the work begun by Nuerhaci and place the third emperor, then a child, on the throne in Peking.[19]

The campaigns and alliances by which this Manchu victory was accomplished were only the outer signs of a process of state formation. These military and diplomatic accomplishments are recorded in detail with all the heroism and skill deployed in the historic records of the period. They are most interesting material. But the clue to this story

[18] *K'ai Kuo Fang Lüeh,* Chapter XXI. Ta Ch'ing was the dynastical name under which the Manchu were to rule over China until 1911.

[19] History given in *K'ai Kuo Fang Lüeh* and Tung Hua Lu. Valuable Outline in Gibert, *op. cit.,* pp. 591 ff., and historical introduction.

of success is to be found in the remarks, scattered in between, on the transformation and political organization of the state. The real greatness of the statesman Nuerhaci and his cooperators and successors was the capacity to create out of different elements and constituents a new organization. The amazing success of a small clan, originally in control of one small frontier state, was due to the ability to blend their own type of life with the Chinese system of the frontier region.

CHAPTER V

___

THE MANCHU FEUDALISM

Feudalism can be defined as a system of relations between lord and vassal, based essentially on land which the vassal held as a fief. The lord recognized the vassal's rights of income and jurisdiction in this fief in exchange for services of a military and general political and financial character. Public functions and private property rights were thus combined in the vassal's fief, while in his relation to the lord public duties had become personal obligations.

In speaking of feudalism we are inclined to think of the European situation as it developed after the collapse of the Roman empire. In this disorderly time the central control over provinces and regions broke up into a number of local powers. The character of these local powers was far from uniform. Some of them were local troop commanders or civil magnates, others were the chiefs of Germanic groups whose invasion had helped to bring the collapse of the former order of things. They became attached to the land, and we know how this combination of the Germanic idea of tribal followership with the surviving territorial civilization created the basis of the central European feudalism of the coming centuries. The insecurity of the time forced free men and small farmers to seek the protection and support of greater landowners and lords and thus furthered the institution of feudal power. They received this protection in exchange for their services and dues. The lord organized from his feudal dependents a private army and extended his jurisdiction over all the inhabitants of his fief. The development was completed when the king recognized the situation and made the lords quasi-representatives of the state. A whole hierarchy of vassalship was then developed with mutual obligations of loyalty, protection and service binding all ranks.

When this feudalism as a political system was finally undermined in different degrees by a growing centralization of administration, its property relations survived much longer than the form of government.

In this European situation feudalism had thus been the result of a former bureaucratic administration breaking up and being partly superseded by tribal groups. In China, in the pre-imperial era before Tsin Shih Huang Ti, feudalism had been of a somewhat different nature. It had been a stage of development from a primitive to a more advanced form of life and not the result of a collapse of a former central order. Consequently it had seen a far more uniform development than in Europe with various deviating features.[1]

But the frontier feudalism of later time, such as the Manchu feudalism, was in its origin more similar to the European picture. The Manchu feudalism was also formed by a tribal society that had become settled on land with a growing importance of agriculture. It was the fringe of the Chinese agricultural bureaucratic system that became superseded by feudalism. The first public functions of the formerly tribal groups were executed in these regions in the form of feudal service and protection. Rival feudal leaders fought among themselves for predominance. And the chief who succeeded in gaining this predominance did so at the head of feudal supporters. He recognized their feudal position and extended it by rewards. The chiefs' own relationship to the neighboring bureaucratic Chinese government was also feudal. The Chinese emperor was the suzerain of the feudal king.

Later, when penetrating further into China, this feudal system was slowly undermined by the establishment step by step of an administration that dealt with the growing state tasks. And again, as also in Europe, when feudalism thus

[1] The Chinese dependence on irrigated agriculture with its necessity for the allotment of water rights and labor etc. necessitated even under feudal conditions a greater employment of clerks than in European feudalism. Compare Owen Lattimore, *op. cit.*, pp. 375/6. For the whole Chinese development see Wittfogel's " Foundations and Stages of Chinese Economic History,' 1935. Also *Liao*, section XIII.

became hollow, the property relations survived longer than the form of government.

Yet we cannot draw the parallel too far. The irrigated agriculture created a kind of feudalism that was very different from the Western form.[2] The kinship system introduced also a special element in the Manchu organization that differed from European conditions. And the military organization of the Manchus was a unique feature that greatly facilitated the smooth transformation from feudalism to bureaucracy.

*　　*　　*

Manchu feudalism had its chief root in the development of frontier agriculture on a smaller scale than the intensive irrigational agriculture of the Chinese type. Human labor was needed, however, for this agriculture too. For a militant group this labor would be subject labor of war prisoners or subjugated peoples. The outstanding and leading Manchus became nobles and their work was done for them by serfs. Serfs were used not only for agricultural labor, but also as artisans and for the manifold activities in housework and accounting.[3] These serfs were not real slaves to be sold at

[2] The greater care necessary for the cultivation of land results in a different position of the serf in irrigated agriculture and eliminates statute labor on the lords fields, replacing it with dues in kind. See Wittfogel, " Die Theorie der Orientalischen Gesellschaft," pp. 96 f.

[3] For the same reason as in note 1 slave labor in the Roman sense is unpractical in irrigated agriculture. See Wittfogel, " Die Theorie der Orientalischen Gesellschaft," pp. 96/7. Otte, *op. cit.,* compares the Manchu system with the high stage of home production as found with the Greeks and Romans. He follows Werner Sombart's analysis of the Greco-Roman economy. And he proposes to use Sombart's term " oikoseconomy " (Oikenwirtschaft) also for the Manchus. He cites Bücher's description of oikos economy: " All the bondage workers of a rich Roman house consisted of two groups, the *familia rustica* and the *familia urbana*. The *familia rustica* was for productive requirements. . . . The *familia urbana* may be divided into administrative personel and indoor and outdoor personel, serving the master and the mistress of the house." There is doubtless a parallel with the subdivision of the bondserfs of the Manchus. In the household they had also a small number of slaves. This comparison seems, however, not too helpful and cannot be carried further. Otte himself mentions that the Manchu serf could not be " sold in the open market." This fact together

will and with whom the master could deal as he liked. The master was on the contrary responsible to the chief for the welfare and adequate care of all the people under his control including the serfs.

But not all the Manchus were nobles, or as to that, serfs. A great number were free men, who were the followers of Manchu nobles; men who at the outset of the Manchu rise did not control serfs themselves.[4] Their number was constantly reinforced by newcomers from the Juchen hinterland.

At the head of this group of feudal nobles was an overlord as chief of the state. We have described how Nuerhaci had become the feudal chief of the Manchu state. His position had a double sanction. He had inherited his rule from his father, an inheritance which by the way did not go by necessity to the eldest son but to the most worthy of the sons' generation. The inherited position was, secondly, confirmed by the Ming emperor through the Chinese officials.[5] This confirmation was given by appointment and the conveyance of a seal, the sign of office. But the loyalty to the emperor of China as suzerain depended on the political situation and became later only nominal.

For his feudal group Nuerhaci was as chief and overlord the highest source of governmental power. And when he took the title of Khan (1616), Nuerhaci indicated that he extended his power over all the other feudal groups too. He had become the head of the feudal hierarchy of the frontier. But this feudal power of Nuerhaci and his successors was modified by a special factor: the clan, the original nomad-tribal family compact that had been carried over into the feudal society. And as with former barbarian dynasties,[6] the conflict between the monarchical and the

with the master's responsibility for the well-being of his dependents indicates the feudal relationship of the serfs in the case of the Manchus with their oriental irrigated agriculture in contrast to the monetary or "capitalist" system of antiquity.

[4] But had a chance to acquire them. Compare the many gifts of prisoners given to simple men in the army as mentioned in the *K'ai Kuo Fang Lüeh*.

[5] See *K. K. F. L.*, Chapter I, p. 1 f.

[6] See our Chapter II on the struggle in Liao history within the ruling family. (Wittfogel-Feng, *Liao*, XIII.) We use here occasionally the term

clan group principal of control showed itself in early Manchu history. It will be discussed at a later time.

In the historical narration of the Manchu rise can be found a number of evidences for this feudal organization. The importance and wealth of a lord or nobleman depended on his ownership of land, horses, cattle and his control of serfs. There was apparently no obstacle to the rise of a free man by merit to the position of nobleman. And the nobleman would be ambitious to extend his position. Consequently the reward given by the chief to the nobles would be in this line. In the narrative of these rewards, important enough to be mentioned in the annals, one can therefore best check the structure of the feudal organization.

The material for these rewards would be gained by wars and raids into the neighboring territories, particularly the Chinese region.[7] But the story of the Manchu rise relates at first a number of fights within the narrower Manchu group itself. It was a fight for control, not for booty. That remained the same when feudal neighbors became involved. These fights would not lead to subjection of formerly free people of the larger Tungus family. When such related people or towns were conquered in the petty fights of Nuerhaci's first years, as a rule the opposing leader or leaders were killed, and the group joined under the rule of Nuerhaci. The serfs and possessions of the nobles that had been killed may have been gained by the conqueror. But on the whole their social structure remained intact. Sometimes even the opposing leader was forgiven after his defeat, when Nuerhaci either did not yet feel strong enough to include the group outright, or when he really expected a loyal, submissive attitude.[8]

"clan" for kinship-group. In the Liao volume, Wittfogel has shown that the Mongol-Tungus tribal world did not know "clans" in the strict sense of the word, but rather loose kinship groups. For certain purposes, however, Wittfogel uses the term "clan," and we follow his example. The problem for the Manchus will be dealt with later in Chapter VII.

[7] Compare Cheng Hsiao-Chin's report in the conclusion of Chapter I, K. K. F. L.

[8] Examples in K. K. F. L., Chapter II.

Thus when the Hata were conquered, their chief or
" beile " (" beile " was the Mongol and Juchen-Manchu
word for chief), Menggebulu by name was at first only
deprived of his position, but received financial support.
Later, when rebellion was feared, he was killed. But when
the Ming interfered, his son Ulgudai was restored to power
and married to a daughter of Nuerhaci, in order to keep him
loyal. The Hata nation perished, however, in the political
strife between their neighbors on both sides and their plight
was made worse by famine. Their remnants joined the
Manchus. When Ulgudai sought refuge with the Manchus,
he received from Nuerhaci " fields, houses, families, clothes
and all sorts of utensils." [9]

Once the control over the Manchu tribes was firmly established and the fight carried further into the neighboring
Chinese regions, more and more is reported of booty in the
form of prisoners and animals.[10] Submitting people were
still taken in without change of their status. But prisoners
were divided among the men of the army.[11] Thus the state
grew by a growth of the feudal organization. Nobles, who
were successful in war or who came to submit received new
fields, families and serfs in smaller and greater numbers.
Free men who distinguished themselves were treated in the
same way. Serfs were given as rewards, serfs were taken
away as punishment. Ever again the narrative mentions
something like: the ruler " presented him of men forty
families," [12] " he gave them official posts, and to each slaves
and servants, cows and horses, fields and huts, clothes and
utensils," [13] " he presented each of the eight heads with 20
men and women, 10 horses and 10 cows, . . . fields, huts
. . .," [14] " the chiefs who had come for homage, were divided into two classes for the reception of gracious gifts;
those belonging to the first class received 10 men and women,

[9] K. K. F. L., Chapter III, Hauer, p. 33.
[10] K. K. F. L., Chapter III at several occasions, Chapter IV and from then
on frequently.
[11] K. K. F. L., Chapter IV, Hauer, pp. 47/8.
[12] K. K. F. L., Chapter V.
[13] Ibid.   [14] Ibid.

10 horses and 10 cows and 50 garments; those of the second class 5 men and women, five horses and five cows and three garments; fields, huts and utensils were made available." [15] These examples could be further extended.

The constant reservoir of captured people, prisoners of war and animals was divided up among the chief's own group and those feudal groups who came to join under Manchu leadership. The state grew by the junction (Kuei 歸) or submission ("pacification") of more and more feudal groups. Through addition of booty in serfs and animals, through the new cultivation of more and more land, it became richer and stronger. On several occasions the necessity of grain storage was mentioned by Nuerhaci.[16] Already the importance of a strong population was clearly realised and emphasized.[17] The constant campaigns into the Ju-chen hinterland, bringing easy laurels to some Nuer-haci's relatives and other nobles, were chiefly organized to gain greater manpower of the same racial stock. The policy of increasing the population was further stressed by the official measures—including financial support—to secure wives for all men without families.[18] The task of finding wives for the serfs was also part of the responsibility of the nobles.

This feudal state slowly expanded into the Chinese agricultural basin were it came to face new administrative problems. This eventually meant the end of feudalism as the political basis of the state. But at first this penetration, bringing a tremendous increase in manpower and agricultural production, brought feudalism to a head and created a powerful group of leading nobles. The position of a noble in the group depended on his income. The size of the income was determined by the control of land and labor gained as rewards for his services. In time a scale of such income was developed. In a speech to discontented Chinese

---

[15] *K. K. F. L.*, Chapter VI (people of the Hurha).
[16] Hauer, *K. K. F. L.*, pp. 10, 42, 53; *K. K. F. L.*, Chapters, I, III, IV, etc.
[17] *K. K. F. L.*, Chapter IV, Hauer, p. 52.
[18] *K. K. F. L.*, Chapter III, p. 41, when over 1000 girls and women were given in marriage.

followers in 1634 T'ai-tsung mentioned that the Manchus had no official money salaries like the Chinese, but had built up a whole system of rewards, where the highest officials (or nobles) had over a thousand serfs, the others less by degrees, according to their rank.[19] On this occasion it can then be learned from the statement of T'ai-tsung that not only the Manchus (Juchen) and Mongols, but even Chinese officials deserting to the Manchus were rewarded in a similar way. Their highest families had not less than 1000 serfs while those of the lowest class had at least 20.[20]

It is very difficult to determine to what degree exactly Chinese in Manchu service were incorporated into this feudal system. We shall deal in the following chapter with the introduction of bureaucratic government by the Manchus. And it will be seen that Chinese and the Chinese basin in Manchuria after its conquest were governed by the Manchus more or less in the Chinese (military) bureaucratic form. But there are also a number of indications that Chinese officials in the Manchu service had likewise become feudal masters and had acquired a great number of serfs and servants in personal bondage. Something of this development may have taken place before the desertion of these Chinese into the Manchu camp.[21] Yet one cannot say that such feudalisation before the Manchus took over had gone far enough to change the essential character of Chinese military bureaucracy. The latter was still strong enough to be respected by the Manchus at the time of the first important desertion of a Chinese official.

In May 1618 the Chinese commander of Fushun, Li Yung-

[19] *K. K. F. L.,* Chapter XVIII, p. 3.

[20] *K. K. F. L.,* Chapter XVIII, p. 5. It should be remembered, however, that in the T'ang period the Chinese aristocracy in China, holding many official positions, was still supported by taxes figured on the basis of a number of families ranging from 300 up to 10,000 according to the aristocratic rank of the official.

[21] The easiness of these desertions after the first military successes of the Manchus has been mentioned before (Chapter IV, p. 44). An indication, mentioned in *K. K. F. L.,* Chapter XV, page 23, that the Liaotung Chinese had become more feudalised than the rest of the Chinese basin will be discussed in Chapter VI, p. 73/74.

fang had surrendered to the Manchus, setting an example to be followed by many later. He and the Chinese people of the several towns and places that surrendered with him were transplanted into Manchurian territory. But their administration remained allegedly bureaucratic, and "higher and lower officials were appointed according to the regulations of the Ming." As an indication of the beginning of the feudalization of these Chinese one may adduce perhaps the fact that Li Yung-fang, who remained their highest official, received a grand-daughter of Nuerhaci as wife.[22]

The first direct mention of feudal status for former Chinese officials under the Manchus was in July 1619. After the further Manchu penetration into Chinese territory, a number of Chinese lower military officials surrendered, following the example of a Mongol formerly in the Chinese service. The Mongol received 100 men, 100 cows, horses, sheep, 5 camels, silver and cloth. The Chinese officials according to rank from 40 to 50 men, 40 to 50 horses, cows and sheep, 1 to 2 camels, silver and cloth. In addition they were all given "women, servants, cows, horses (for their men?), fields, huts and utensils."[23] This then was clearly a beginning of feudal positions for Chinese officials in Manchu service, a development that in 1634, the year of the above mentioned speech of T'ai-tsung, had gone so much further.

Up to then a great number of Chinese had surrendered. Some rebellious troop leaders had come of their own accord. In the first case of troops surrendering the rank and file was partly divided among their own former officers and the rest was given to the Manchu nobles.[24] A quasi-feudal relationship must have been thus developed in these cases among the Chinese themselves. In the case of the rebel leaders it developed in the group itself without any such assignments. One has thus the picture of Chinese quasi-feudalism within the Manchu organization.

It is, of course, open to speculation how much by this

[22] See annex, Li Yung-fangs biography.
[23] *K. K. F. L.*, Chapter VI, p. 86.
[24] *K. K. F. L.*, Chapter XV; Hauer, *K. K. F. L.*, p. 295.

process Chinese were converted to a feudal way of life, or to what extent Manchu feudalism became diluted by taking Chinese into its body. Apparently most of the Chinese officials had serfs belonging to them, working for them, who could be inherited by their descendants. Yet, when they came to the Manchu side, they brought with them their idea of offices and administration, of which the next chapter will deal. Genuine feudalism means, however, a lifelong and bequeathable position of government and control over dependent people on agricultural land in exchange for loyal followership. It seems that the Chinese officials never had enjoyed quite this position. Their administrative position was not hereditary,[25] and in most cases they could not only be transferred, displaced or promoted as in any bureaucratic system, but their governmental functions were altogether delegated and not original. They acted under the orders and control of several government offices and not as feudal masters.

On the other hand these newly created government offices that came with the Chinese and of which the next chapter will deal, undermined also the feudal position of the Manchu nobles. For them too the administrative job became more important than the original feudal position. What remained was the benefit of the work of serfs, not the political control. In this latter benefit the Chinese members of the Manchu group seem to have participated. But it was no longer genuine political feudalism. Thus Chinese bureaucracy with feudal characteristics and government controlled Manchu feudalism met each other half way.

The growth of administration that finally ended the political importance of feudalism did not come only from outside. The greater the power of the feudal lords and their control over people and land became, the more they needed themselves a growing administration in their own fiefs. Diversification of activity became necessary and clerks were

[25] Compare annex, the end of Li Yung-fangs biography about the career of Li's sons.

needed that could deal with the new tasks confronting the nobles who had become great landowners.

It has been mentioned already that the serfs were not only used for work in the fields by their masters. Many of them were warriors for most of the time. But others helped also in administration, were artisans, or even scholars. This diversification was encouraged by the ruler. Nuerhaci ordered the Manchu clan nobles to use their people in the right way. Whoever was efficient in war should not be forced into other services. For secret state affairs careful and thorough people should be used.[26] This division of work seems to have been particularly used to create a class of clerks. When later the state needed learned men for its growing bureaucratic administration, it found them among the serfs of the feudal nobles. Thus an examination of (Confucian) scholars was ordered: " The Beile and Manchurian, Chinese and Mongol families, who possess scholars as their property shall have those examined. For each chosen they shall be compensated with another man." [27]

When bureaucracy developed in the Manchu state there was thus a competition between central government and feudal masters for the control of the essential services. At the outset the necessary national or common tasks were divided among the leading nobles by assessment of the labor or expenses involved. A description of some assessments of services and products for national tasks was given in T'ai-tsung's own words on the occasion of his admonition to discontented Chinese officers mentioned above. The regular services were shared by all, with the Chinese complaining of a comparatively high burden. To demonstrate that the Manchu did not get off lighter than the Chinese, T'ai-tsung enumerated in detail the Manchu nobles' services rendered in campaigns, for guards, for communications, for artisans and clerks, the delivery of products like horses, corn, game,

[26] *K. K. F. L.,* Chapter V, p. 4.
[27] *K. K. F. L.,* Chapter XII, p. 12.   This edict was published in 1629. Hauer in his translation omits the word " Chinese." Yet the inclusion of Chinese families among those possessing scholar " serfs " is another important evidence of " feudalism " among the Chinese in Manchu service.

the relinquishment of land etc.[28] These assessments were assigned to the Manchu nobles exclusively whenever war, the inclusion of new groups, embassies, news communication, patrol and other military preparation made them necessary.

The method of assessment for public purposes and the responsibility of the nobles for their people remained even after a more complicated central administration had been created. The latter was ingrafted on the feudal basis without immediately dissolving it. As the feudal lords had developed their own clerical administration, a certain friction between feudal and public interests frequently arose. The central government under the ruler would attempt to limit and keep in check the great power of the feudal lords so that it would not become dangerous for the unity of the state. One way of doing this was to see that they used their own power only in a way that would not be harmful to the public interest. The state regarded their position of control over people as much a responsibility of the holder as a privilege. Those who had neglected the people they had to care for were punished.

In particular this conflict of interests became apparent in the case of the leading feudal nobles, "beile" as they were called,[29] who were mostly princes of the imperial clan. It is told how they were kept from private jurisdiction.[30] They had to be admonished not to take private booty,[31] not to abuse their domain administration or to be idle or pleasure seeking. They were stopped from exploiting their dependent people too crassly by excessive forced labor.[32] In time of famine they were ordered to give corn to the needy, free

[28] *K. K. F. L.,* Chapter XVIII, p. 4.

[29] The term "beile," as has been mentioned before, is a Mongol-Manchu word for chief. The word is the same as the Turkish "boila" (prince) and has even come into Slavonic languages. See T. Marquart, "Die Chronologie der alttürkischen Inschriften." Leipzig, 1898, S. 41. (Quoted from E. Hauer, (Prince Dorgon). In the case of the Manchus the title was given to the outstanding members of the imperial clan, after Nuerhaci had taken for himself the title Khan or Emperor. According to the later court order a beile was a prince of third rank.

[30] *K. K. F. L.,* Chapter V, pp. 7/8.

[31] *K. K. F. L.,* Chapter VIII, p. 28.   [32] *K. K. F. L.,* Chapter XX, p. 14.

if necessary,[33] and not to enrich themselves by storing grain,[34] not to raise corn prices for their own advantage and exploit thus their position as the greatest grain producers to the public disadvantage.[35] These limitations were mostly but the economic sphere of a struggle for the control of the state that was chiefly fought out in the field of political and military affairs. Particularly through the new military organization the feudal power was broken.

Originally all feudal lords had in military affairs the command over their followers and serfs and led them in war. But with the growing army a military organization that was based on greater unity became necessary. Thus Nuerhaci created the Manchu banner organization.[36] Most, but not all of the feudal characteristics of the army disappeared with it. Some of the so-called Niroo, subunits of the banners, remained under the command of hereditary leaders.[37] And some of the subdivisions were formed by complete groups of bondserfs of the leading nobles of the imperial family.[38] And furthermore feudalism or tribalism survived of course in the main part of the auxiliary Mongol troops. But with these exceptions the army which we will describe in detail later, became bureaucratic in its organization.

But the political control of the army did not yet belong to the newly developing central government, for each banner of the army was at the outset given to a prince of the imperial family. These princes or beiles came to control thus not only great numbers of serfs and land, but also temporarily in an hereditary feudal way the otherwise bureaucratic military banner organization. This gave these few princes

[33] *K. K. F. L.*, Chapter XXII, p. 18.
[34] *K. K. F. L.*, Chapter XXII, p. 18; XXIV, p. 4.
[35] *K. K. F. L.*, Chapter XXIV, p. 5.
[36] See next chapter.
[37] Compare Chapter III, section on Manchurian banner organization, обстоятельное описание происхождения и состояния маньджурскаго народа и войска в осми знаменах состоящаго. (Russian translation of *Pa-ch'i T'ung-chih*).
[38] The so-called Pao I (包衣). See later Chapter VI, note 14.

a feudal position of extraordinary political might, as the
banners were the Manchu people's organization for peace
and war. They came, however, to this position as members
of the imperial clan and not because of their feudal power.
A third element, the clan power, was thus reintroduced
into the general struggle between feudalism and bureaucracy for the organization of the Manchu state. This question of the political control of the banners by members of
the imperial clan will therefore be discussed later in connection with the importance of the clan element in the
Manchu state. First we shall describe the banner organization itself, as the banners were the institution in which the
question as to what clanism, feudalism and bureaucracy
would play in the Manchu state, was decided. The bureaucratic system prevailed, and with this the next chapter
will deal.

CHAPTER VI

MANCHU BUREAUCRACY

When the Manchus penetrated from the valleys of the Long White Mountains into the larger plains of the Chinese basin the feudal organization no longer sufficed as the integrating factor of the state. Feudalism was effective as long as the community lived on scattered patches of agricultural land in separated mountain valleys. The agricultural plains did not have any natural frontiers for the separation of feudal powers; the common tasks of defense, of irrigation and flood prevention became larger, and a centralized system to allot services and expenses for the whole community became indispensable. This of necessity lead to a weakening of the authority and responsibility of local lords and chiefs in favor of a system of departments or bureaus carrying on the business of government by appointed officials.

It has been stated before how former dynasties which came from the frontier had to deal with this problem of developing in the place of the powers of the local chiefs an administrative apparatus that would be directed from a central government. The difficulty of this transformation and the ensuing dualism have been mentioned. The Manchus did not encounter difficulties to quite the same extent. Their transformation from feudalism to bureaucracy, though not without frictions, was smoother than it had been in the past. What made it smoother was the kind of military organization which the Manchus set up early in this development: the banners.

These banners had their model in the military district organization of the Ming, the Wei, described above. Nuerhaci's farsighted adaptation of a similar organization for the Manchus was the most decisive step of the Manchu penetration into China.

At the outset it was certainly not clear to Nuerhaci how far his start would carry him in the end. Had he only planned to secure for himself his fathers position and the chieftaincy of the Chien-chow district, he could have carried on with the feudal system. But his initial successes and the resistance he had found made him envision the ambitious scheme of creating a strong frontier power including his neighbors. Once started there was no given limit to this extension. His ambition grew to the vague and limitless claim of founding a great "Yeh" (業), family realm or state. This aim surpassed the capacity of the inherited feudal system. With it in mind Nuerhaci founded the banner organization even before the penetration of the Chinese basin had begun.

The first step was taken in 1601, immediately after the inclusion of the first neighboring people, the Hata. "As the number of followers had grown extensively" Nuerhaci divided the army into new units.[1] And these units showed the first definite signs of bureaucratic administration.

The history of the Manchu army can be traced back into the pre-feudal time. In this period the kinsmen from villages or boroughs marched together on hunting trips or campaigns. A group of about ten men chose their own leader by taking out an arrow. The word "Niroo," Ju-chen for arrow, became thus the name for the military unit.[2] The name "Niroo" remained when this elective system disappeared in the feudal period. The feudal lord acquired his position by birth, and smaller feudal lords would follow the leadership of a major chief.[3] However, a major feudal chief like Nuerhaci, did also appoint commanders over Niroo units. The first such appointments are reported from the year 1584, when two

[1] K. K. F. L., Chapter III, p. 6.
[2] Ibid.
[3] The system was, however, rather flexible and it happened frequently that followers left their chief to join the group of another chief or even aspired themselves for the chieftaincy. Compare the story of Nikan Wailan, who had been the follower of Nuerhaci's father, before his connivance with the Chinese and rivalry to Nuerhaci. K. K. F. L., Chapter I, p. 3. Compare also the attitude taken at this occasion by the descendants of the Ninguta Beile.

former enemy warriors received the command over 300 men each.[4] Appointments of this kind indicated that the feudal followership was beginning to be transformed into an army with appointed officers. In 1601 the whole Manchu army was divided into Niroos of 300 men each with appointed officers who received the title Commander of a Niroo or Niroo-ejen.[5]

These appointments marked a new kind of government. This becomes even clearer from the fact that the new military organization was initiated by a registration of people. Shortly before the families of the newly subjected Hata had been registered in records.[6] And on many occasions from that time on we read that newly subjected families were grouped together and recorded, so that we can conclude that these records were a general institution for all the people. The recording meant evidently a direct central control over all the people regardless of allegiance to feudal lords. The recording then was connected with the military organization when in the coming years larger units were formed. Five Niroos were called a " Jalan" and placed under one higher commander. Five Jalans formed a " Banner," the military unit for which the Manchus became so famous. At first the army consisted of four such banners. In 1615 the development was completed by the creation of four more banners, so that there were now eight in all.[7] Together with the Banners came the banner lists, the records in which all the members of the banners, their names, appointments and all personal affairs were noted. In peace and war these banners became the administrative organization of the Manchu people, and through the appointed officers this people followed the rule of a central bureaucracy.

It has been said that this banner organization of the Manchus was something new and different from the system used by either Mongol or Tungus former invaders of China. How then did the Manchus happen to come by it? The

---

[4] K. K. F. L., Chapter I; Hauer, K. K. F. L., p. 13.
[5] K. K. F. L., Chapter III, p. 6.
[6] K. K. F. L., Chapter III, p. 5.   [7] K. K. F. L., Chapter IV, pp. 16 f.

answer is that Nuerhaci had before him the Chinese military guards and posts instituted under the Ming. The army he created resembled the Ming system in so many ways that it can hardly have been accidental.

Like the Wei of the Ming, the banners became a civil as well as a military organization for all Manchu people. The registration of the banner people in banner lists reminds one of the registration lists of the Chinese Wei as mentioned above. Here like there a military bureaucracy dealt not only with command in war time but with civil affairs as well. The men of the Chinese Wei lived in assigned regions where they produced enough to support themselves. The banner units became settled in the same way. As a matter of fact the settling of peoples in military units at strategic places with the additional task of cultivating new land became one of the basic policies of the Manchus.

Yet there was a difference between the Chinese and Manchu policy. The Chinese Wei were organized regionally. Each Wei formed a certain district bordering on others. In this regional attachment lay a danger of local policy with local interests that would facilitate a breakup of Chinese control in times of crisis.[8] The Chinese, organising a free settled agricultural population for local defense, had to run the risk of such regionalism. The Manchus were in a somewhat different position. It is most likely that the Manchus with their surviving feudalism were more aware of the danger of regionalism. They were also very much more mobile. Agriculture was still being extended and new land brought under cultivation. It was thus neither necessary nor desirable to give one group exclusive control over a newly included region. And it became a policy to settle in a certain place not one complete military unit, but rather fractions of several military units. The peoples of the same banner became thus scattered in several regions, and in a

[8] Thus after the fall of Liaoyang, which was the capital of a Wei, all the remaining towns of this Wei, over 70 in number, surrendered likewise. And the history of the fall of Talingho and the Manchus' dealing with the Chinese officers that surrendered in this town shows that they were regarded as one political clique with one interest.

given region people of several banners could be found. On one occasion it is for example reported that ten people of each Niroo were settled on land to be newly cultivated, each group in a village with sixteen officials and eight clerks to place to account the entries and expenses.[9] The banners did thus have their agrarian basis as had the Chinese Wei, but they were more scattered than their Chinese counterpart.

As for the rest, the parallel can be drawn rather closely. The banners organized the whole Manchu people in peace as well as in war. Production, taxes, services and assessments of the people became regulated in this frame. A staff of clerks figured out the amount of work and production within the banner units themselves and for the general public purpose.[10] The banner was simply the administrative unit of the state,[11] as the Wei was the administrative unit for the Ming. Both banner and Wei were bureaucratic in administrative form, both selfsupporting, both primarily military, but both of necessity included the civil, economic and other activities of the people registered in the unit. Even the use of a flag as sign for a unit occurred on both sides, the Chinese and the Manchu, although this was certainly nothing so very unusual. In the Chinese organization the smaller units were called banners. Each "Post" consisted of two "general banners" and ten "small banners."[12] The Manchu used the term banner for the largest unit.[13]

Still, if the Manchu banner formed a parallel to the Chinese Wei and—as we think—was largely copied from it, the Chinese and the Manchus had come to a similar thing

[9] *K. K. F. L.,* Chapter IV, p. 12.

[10] Serf service was thereby in no way excluded, as the economic basis of feudalism survived. Each official or officer, for instance all the Niroo commanders, had their serfs to work for them.

[11] Compare A. O. Mayer's Chinese Government, No. 28, on the banners.

[12] 總旗 and 小旗. See Hauer, *K. K. F. L.,* Chapter I, note 53, with a description of the Ming system quoted from Tze Yuan Shen, 159.

[13] The use of a real banner as sign for the lead of the army was known to the Manchus already at the time of their first wars against the Hulun states. One black silk banner was carried with the army as a rallying and also a religious symbol. Thus one reads that Nuerhaci offered a great sacrifice to this banner at the beginning of a campaign. *K. K. F. L.,* Chapter IV, p. 2.

from two different approaches. The Chinese Wei was a partial devolution from normal bureaucracy, the Manchu banner the beginning of evolution towards bureaucracy. If the two met in the middle of the road, their different origins explain their differences in character. The officers of the banners were officials who could be replaced and promoted, and a staff of clerks was needed for the accounting and the division of the services. But at the same time there remained in the banner certain feudal and clan relations and elements. Most of the high officials chosen to command and administer the banner must have been the leading feudal lords, a high percentage of them from the imperial clan. Their serfs were included in the banners, so that one finds free Niroos and serf Niroos side by side.[14] The still more important question of the political control of the banners played an important part in the struggle between imperial clan and emperor for power and will be dealt with later.

The banner administration was created as a preparation for the coming struggle before the Manchus crossed the frontier region and invaded the Chinese basin. This preparation included other institutions of a bureaucratic state. While the banners and their officials represented the local administration, the central government received also appointed secretaries of state. In 1616 the offices of five High Government Secretaries and ten Executive Secretaries were created. The state secretaries had been raised from the " ordinary people " and placed in their high position.[15] They were the predecessors of the later six Pu or ministries copied from China. Their functions were however not only those of ministers, they also acted as court to decide legal cases.

The final challenge to China was made in the same year, 1616, by the acceptance by the ruler, " on the demand " of his nobles and officials, of the title of emperor and the founding of a dynasty. It was a Chinese type of dynasty, with a Chinese name for the period of the reign: T'ien Ming–

[14] The so-called " pao i," 包衣, compare Mayer, *The Chinese Government*, No. 379.
[15] *K. K. F. L.*, Chapter XIV, p. 7.

Heaven Ordered; with a Chinese title for the dynasty: Hou Chin or Late Chin, indicating that the dynastic claim of the former Chin dynasty was taken up again.[16] The inauguration speeches were full of allusions to the Confucian conception of the state.[17]

With an emperor ruler, two grades of bureaucratic state secretaries as central government, and the territorial military organization of the banners a bureaucratic Manchu state had thus come into being, ready for a fight with Chinese Manchuria.

The Manchu feudal nobles were however at the outset not trained for bureaucratic administration. The Manchus had therefore not only to imitate the Chinese system, but also to use Chinese for their administrative posts. There were many such posts to be filled and more and more people were needed for them. In many instances the ruler was searching after talented men for his growing administration.[18] And he was pointing out that not kinship or social position but talent were to be taken as conditions for appointments; an emphasis clearly necessary at the time of transformation from feudalism and clanship to bureaucracy. But the "talented" Manchus were not enough. And thus Chinese serfs of the feudal lords were taken for this purpose. It was mentioned in the last chapter that scholar-serfs were thus exchanged against other men.

This draft of scholar-serfs indicates the beginning of a system that could have led to a slave administration as built up by the Osmanlis in the Ottoman state in the 14th century[19]—a system where the actual administration was

---

[16] The dynastical name was Hou Chin—Late Chin, in reference to the Chin dynasty of the Juchen that had reigned over Manchuria and Northern China from 1115-1234. The name was in 1636 changed into Ta Ch'ing, the name under which the Manchu dynasty ruled over China until 1911. In the dynastic histories we find the name Manchu instead Hou Chin for the early time. We know, however, that this is a falsification started in 1636 in order to disconnect the Manchu dynasty with the defeated former Chin, and to start with a clear sheet. Compare Gibert, *op. cit.,* p. 60.

[17] *K. K. F. L.,* Chapter IV, pp. 2 ff.

[18] *K. K. F. L.,* Chapter IV; Hauer, p. 54, etc.

[19] Compare The Osmanli in Toynbee, a *Study of History,* Vol. III, pp.

in the hands of trained alien people who were serfs, or in the case of the Osmanlis rather slaves, and therefore absolutely dependent upon the ruler.[20] For the Manchus this system was, however, only a start that did not develop further. With the later inclusion of greater groups of Chinese—no longer as prisoners but as part of the nation on equal terms—the Chinese official assured himself a position with his own rights similar to the one he enjoyed under the Chinese rule. The Manchus wanted to win the Chinese over. This they could not do by the formation of a slave administration. They needed the help of experienced Chinese officials on terms which these officials could and would accept.

This broader policy towards the Chinese which in its result decisively changed and shaped the new Manchu state came with the invasion of the Chinese basin. It was a deliberate far-sighted policy of Nuerhaci and was a development which we want to follow up in detail with regard to its important initial step.

The first attack on the Chinese basin in 1618 was not meant as an occupation. The aim was the destruction of the Chinese town of Fushun that barred to the Manchus the approach into the Chinese basin. After this aim was achieved the Manchus withdrew again from Chinese territory because they were then not yet strong enough to hold it against the expected Chinese counterblow. But they gained something more than the destruction of the town. The Chinese major in command of Fushun, Li Yung-fang, surrendered with the people of his town, and the people of the smaller towns Tungchow and Mahatan and a number of other boroughs and military posts followed his example.

It was the first such desertion on the Chinese side, and it was to set an example for many Chinese officials to follow in the years to come. The story of Li Yung-fang seems

22-50, with references to Lybyer, *The Government of the Ottoman Empire in the time of Suliman the Magnificent.*

[20] With the Osmanli the fighting forces themselves consisted of such alien slaves.

therefore of particular interest.[21] Li Yung-fang, a native of
T'iehling in Liaotung, had been at his post at Fushun at
least since 1613, that is five years before the Manchu attack.
In these years he must have become well acquainted with
the Manchus. Besides his official position in which he had
to handle Chinese frontier policy, the regular markets at
Fushun gave ample occasion for such acquaintance. And
considering the nature of Chinese officials and Chinese trade,
he had probably become personally interested in the profit
of trade. It must also have been interesting for him to watch
the developing bureaucracy of the Manchu administration.

In 1613 Li had exchanged letters with Nuerhaci about
the aggressive policy of the Manchus against the Hulun
states. Nuerhaci had come in person to hand over a letter.
Li received him honorably. There is no record of oral discussion at the time, but most likely there was some
personal contact.

When the Manchus marched against Fushun in 1618, a
letter was dispatched to Li intimating a capitulation. There
was the statement that Li "had been always an intelligent
man with a sound grasp of present requirements," hinting
at former understandings between Li and the Manchus. The
letter offers Li admission on par into the Manchu state organization. "Our state has always had a generous apprecia-
tion of talented men. And if somebody is gifted and quick in
administration, we elevate him, appoint him and bind him
by marriage," the letter went on. And Li was told that he
would keep his position and would find protection in the
Manchu state. The protection would be extended to the
Chinese people under Li. The alternative was death, terror
and destruction for all. Again there was the sentence: "But
if you fight, how can our arrows know who you are?"; an
indication that they would take good care to kill him.

This was the type of letter sent later on many occasions
to wavering Ming officials. On the Manchu side it showed
a determined policy to build a larger state. It was not

[21] See his life in *Erh Chen Ch'uan*, I, translation given in annex here.

simple, crude, barbarian invasion, but a well planned political strategy that carried Nuerhaci into Chinese Manchuria.[22]

Li Yung-fang surrendered after initial fighting. It would have been his duty as a Chinese official to die for his emperor if he could not resist the attack. That he surrendered instead is an indication that there was enough motive to do so. He had held his post for several years in succession and had almost certainly acquired local interests in trade and property, which, if left to him, would enable him to remain somebody of importance even without the shadow of the Chinese empire behind him. And the development of the Manchu state with its growing bureaucratic banner and central organization would give him such a chance and a career similar to one in Chinese service. A purely " barbarian " society would scarcely have outweighed the shame of treason for the Chinese official. But the development of the Manchu state had prepared the ground for surrender. Li became a loyal supporter of the Manchu power and resisted all attempts of loyal Chinese officials to win him back to the Chinese cause.

To gain this kind of support the Manchus had to make concessions and to accept the Chinese way of doing things. The slave administration of which certain beginnings existed could not serve this purpose. A new element entered the Manchu state: The Chinese subject and the Chinese official class. At first this element was not very numerous. One thousand families were taken with Li Yung-fang from their former homes into Manchurian territory. But this number was to grow steadily. And with the later conquest of the Chinese basin, the Chinese population must have finally outnumbered considerably the Manchus and Mongols in the Manchu state in Manchuria.

[22] It is for instance interesting to note that after the capture of Fushun Nuerhaci permitted the Chinese merchants from other parts of China that had been in this town when it was attacked, and who were thus captured, to return home. They received money, presents and the Manchu political claims were made known to them before they left. This shows indeed a very farsighted propaganda policy of Nuerhaci. See K. K. F. L., Chapter V; Hauer, K. K. F. L., p. 67.

The Chinese factor changed slowly the original character of the Manchu state, which became more and more predominantly bureaucratic. When Li Yung-fang and the 1000 families were taken in, land, huts, horses, cattle and implements were given to them and they were settled near Yenden in the Chinese way. That is, "as formerly under the Ming, higher and lower officials were appointed," Li Yung-fang, raised to the rank of general (banner-general!), remained their highest commander. He received further the promised Manchu princess as wife and was thus connected by marriage with the Manchu clan.

From that time on one Chinese group after another joined the Manchu state. Most of them were the people and officials of newly conquered towns and regions. Some were Chinese rebels or bandits escaping from China Proper to the Manchu side. But the latter were also groups that originated in Chinese Manchuria.

It should be remembered that the change made in the Manchu state was not quite as sudden and epoch making as it may seem at first. Along the frontier the Chinese had become less Chinese by acculturation to the Manchus; just as the Manchus with their banner organization and bureaucracy had become somewhat acculturated to the Chinese. The change was thus gradual, but nevertheless it was fundamental in its final affect. Formerly the state consisted of the clan people and their serfs. But after the attack on Fushun captured or newly subjected Chinese were not all distributed as slaves or serfs among the leaders, officers and men of the banner army. Instead they were registered as "free subjects."[23] Chinese officials were confirmed in their former positions when they surrendered. In other words the Chinese form of political existence, civil and military bureaucracy, was taken over by the Manchus.

This seems to be a contradiction of what was said before

---

[23] The Chinese term is "Min Hu" (民戶). Compare, for instance, K. K. F. L., Chapter IX, p. 6, where it is used in contrast to "Hu K'ou" (戶口) "people"; and Chapter XI, p. 13, where it is used in contrast to "Nu" (奴), slaves.

about the feudalism and the scale of serf control introduced also for the Chinese officials by the Manchus between 1618 and 1634. The contradiction disappears, if it is realized that the two developments went side by side without a clear line of demarcation and sometimes with one overlapping the other. It may well be that the followers or "subjects" of a Chinese border official had actually become something like his "tribe." It may be, on the other side, that the feudalisation existed more in words than in fact. In the language of imperial addresses the control of Chinese officials over a certain number of families could have been compared to the feudal lordship of the Manchu nobles over their serfs simply in order to emphasize the equality of treatment and position of Manchu and Chinese leaders under the Manchu regime. Nuerhaci as well as his successors were always anxious to emphasize this equality in order to prevent desertions and a breakup of their conglomerate state. Statements of the equality of position of the Chinese and Manchu leaders should therefore be taken *cum grano salis.* The Chinese officials may have often been set over a number of families without the same domination as the feudal lord. And it may even be that both the official-subject and the lord-serf relationship were modified towards a middle course by their juxta-position.

Even so, there remain clear cases both for Chinese feudalism and for preservation of Chinese bureaucracy. For the former the Fifth Chapter has given examples. For the latter there is proof in the frequent recording of the registration of Chinese as "free subjects."[23] Sometimes both Chinese feudalism and bureaucracy appear in the same scene. An interesting case of this kind is recorded at the fall of the town of Talingho in the Chinese basin.[24] On this occasion many Chinese officers and men had surrendered to the Manchus. Of these the higher officers were assigned to the eight banners, four to each banner.[25] Over 100 lower officers

---

[24] *K. K. F. L.,* Chapter XV, p. 23; Hauer, *K. K. F. L.,* p. 288.
[25] They thus became most likely feudal lords with regard to their standing and income while remaining officials in position.

were assigned to former Chinese officials already on the Manchu side, for reception and care. Then the chronicle goes on: "Their men were separated according to their origin from Hotung or Hohsi.[26] The men from Hohsi were reunited with the old Chinese people in the eight banners.[27] Those men from Hotung that had deserted from Liaotung were given back to their masters. Those without masters were given to competent officers for placement." Hotung or Liaotung, the eastern part of the Chinese basin was nearest to the Manchu feudal world, while Liaohsi or Hohsi, the Western part, was further away and nearer to China.[28] The fact that the men from Hohsi after capture by the Manchus became free banner men, while those from Hotung were handed back to former masters or otherwise divided up, would indicate that a differentiation existed already under Chinese rule. In Hohsi—nearer to China but at the same time next to the Mongol regions of Jehol—the Chinese conception of life as "free subjects" had not only survived but been strengthened by the freer life of the neighboring Mongol tribes.[29] While in Hotung—at the edge of the Manchu world—feudalisation had developed already under Chinese rule. Thus the Manchus in taking in the Chinese accepted this difference.

Yet we know of other cases of Liaotung Chinese who became "free subjects" and bannermen under the Manchus, so that we cannot conclude more from the above example than that Chinese feudalism had been stronger in Liaotung than in Liaohsi. And the phenomenon of Chinese feudalism side by side with Chinese bureaucracy in the Manchu

[26] Hotung and Hohsi, same as Liaotung and Liaohsi, means the two parts of Chinese Manchuria: East and West of the Liao River (Ho—river).

[27] This sentence, in Chinese: 以河西人. 歸于八旗舊漢民內, which is so important, is omitted in Hauer's translation!

[28] It was the region where the Ming had established the horse pastures mentioned in Chapter III.

[29] The military frontier bureaucracy of the Wei may in this case have been influenced by the tribal Mongol world, where cattle property gave greater individual freedom. We mentioned before in Chapter III that under the Ming a mixed cattle-agricultural economy had penetrated the Chinese basin of Manchuria from the Mongol side.

state is better understood if we think of the different geographical regions from which the Chinese partisans came.

But the chief importance of the Chinese in the Manchu state was that they furthered bureaucracy and the bureaucratic development and diminished the feudal element in Manchu society. Once the institution of the Chinese " subject " was generally accepted in the Manchu state, it seems that even a retrograde motion of the former distribution of Chinese as serfs happened occasionally. Thus one reads: " As Taitsung now feared that with longer duration of the distribution perhaps oppressions or ill treatment might happen, he ordered that there be given according to the rank of the Manchurian officials, to each Pei Yu—the Tsoling of to-day—(the commander of a Niroo) only eight strong men (of a certain group of formerly captured Chinese villagers who had been distributed as serfs) to be at his disposal. The rest were to be settled separately in villages, registered as subjects, and placed under selected honest and correct Chinese officials." [30]

Thus the Chinese forced their standards on the invader. True, some became "Manchus," but the majority retained while obeying their new masters the Chinese idea of government. Far from being slaves, they could call themselves at the court " ch'en," officials, while the Manchus as a sign of the feudal origin of their obedience addressed themselves as slaves, " nu," in their relationship to the emperor; a distinction which remained after the conquest of China Proper right down to the revolution in 1911.

It was not so difficult for the Manchus to integrate the Chinese into their state. The Chinese Wei, formed for the frontier, had served as model for the Manchu banners. When now the Manchus conquered the Chinese basin, it was comparatively easy to include the Chinese into the Manchu organization. The Chinese formerly belonging to a Wei

[30] *K. K. F. L.*, Chapter IX, p. 6. On the other side the Chinese officials were held responsible for the well being of the group they administered. A simple method was used to find out the efficiency of their administration. If the number of families and people under their care had increased, they were promoted, otherwise degraded or punished.

became now, under the same or newly appointed officials, units of the Manchu army. They became banner units. At first there was only one Chinese banner unit, then two, then four and finally eight, which then became attached to the eight Manchu banners.[31] A separate Chinese unit could thus be found in each Manchu banner.

At the same time the Manchu army itself, that is its Manchu units, became sprinkled with Chinese. Though acculturated to the Manchu life, they must also have had a diluting effect on the original Manchu society and feudal life. Captured Chinese were divided among the Manchu Niroos, and high officers without their Chinese men were placed in Manchu banners.[32] If one remembers that there was constant intermarriage among these groups, it really becomes difficult to say just how many genuine Manchus were left outside the imperial clan itself.[33]

In this form Chinese influence and the growth of the banners made the banner administration more complex. The officials were frequently admonished to practice a careful performance of their duties. [34] But a greater number of officials was needed. In 1626, after Nuerhaci's death, the new emperor reorganized the banner command with one chief, two assistant chiefs for civil affairs and two inspecting secretaries each.[35]

Not only the banner administration needed such an enlargement. The ever increasing size of the Chinese population and the resulting growth and bureaucratization of the banners demanded an extension of the central supervisory bureaucratic authority. The example again was the Chinese administration, now with so many Chinese officials in the Manchu ranks even easier to adopt. In 1631 the Beiles and high officials decided in a meeting to establish the 6 Pu

---

[31] *K. K. F. L.*, Chapter XVII, p. 319; XXI, p. 391; XXIV, p. 452; Chapter XXVII., Hauer, *K. K. F. L.*, p. 489, and Chapter XXXI., Hauer, *K. K. F. L.*, p. 554/5. Mayer's *Chinese Government*, No. 379.
[32] *K. K. F. L.*, Chapter XV, p. 23, see above, note 25 f.
[33] Compare Chapter IX, note 5.
[34] *K. K. F. L.*, Chapter VIII, Hauer, *K. K. F. L.*, pp. 120, 137/8, etc.
[35] *K. K. F. L.*, Chapter IX, Hauer, *K. K. F. L.*, pp. 146 ff.

or ministries, patterned and even named after the example of the Chinese imperial government in Peking. They were the ministries of civil affairs, finances, rites, war, justice and public works.[36] Each had one head, who was in each case a member of the imperial clan, and each had Manchu, Mongol and Chinese directors and advisors. The censorate, the three secretaries' offices and the Mongol office completed the imitation of the Chinese system.[37] The Manchu administration had become essentially an image of the Chinese bureaucratic system.

This account of the bureaucratic development of the Manchu organization should not be concluded without reference to another effect of the Chinese influence on the growing Manchu state. The Chinese officials going over to the Manchus brought with them not only their knowledge of organization but also their respect for rules, discipline and the idea of "Staatsraison," to which a feudal noble had to get accustomed. An incident in the life of Li Yung-fang, the Chinese officer who was the first to surrender to the Manchus, may serve to stress this point.[38] This man, once on the Manchu side, remained loyal to his new master. With the exception of the defense against the first great Ming counter attack right after the battle in which he surrendered he took part in the fighting against his former Chinese comrades and in the campaigns against the Chinese basin. The Ming officers sent many letters asking him to return. He handed them to his new ruler together with the messengers. His most active participation in the shaping of events was, however, in the campaign against Korea. The Manchu emperor had directed that Korea be brought to submission, but treated fairly and mildly. The political aim of the campaign was the assurance of the flank of the new Manchu state. The trained Chinese official must have seen and understood this, in contrast to at least one of the leading Manchu lords of the imperial clan who could not think beyond his

---

[36] *K. K. F. L.*, Chapter XIV, Hauer, *K. K. F. L.*, pp. 258 ff.
[37] *K. K. F. L.*, Chapters XXI, p. 392; XXII, pp. 403-4; XXV, pp. 469-70.
[38] See annex.

personal enrichment in an old time looting raid. After the
Manchu army had penetrated Korea, the king of Korea was
ready to submit to and fulfill the proposed conditions. The
Manchu Beile Amin, however, wanted to march on for loot
and the plunder of the capital. With reasonable arguments Li
Yung-fang gained the support of the other Manchu leaders
to the proposed agreement with the king. But Amin reviled
him with the words: "You Chinese slave(!), why all this
talk? I should kill you." Yet Li Yung-fang's moderation won
out, although Amin had to be satisfied with an extra agreement and extra booty, a fact that left for some time a bitter-
ness in the new Manchu-Korean relations. But the Chinese bureaucrat had won over the feudal nobles to the
advantage of the Manchu state.[39]

Most of the important bureaucratic head positions were
kept by the Manchus for their own people. But Chinese
secretaries and councilors introduced the Manchus to this
new type of government. The Chinese tradition and experience was thus gained for the young state. A deliberate
policy of integration was undertaken by the outstanding
Manchu leaders. First among these leaders in the sixteen
thirties and forties was Prince Dorgon who helped to build
this administration. When the ministries were created, this
man became minister of civil affairs, certainly the most
important administrative post in the Manchu organization.
As such he had the best opportunity to become acquainted with
the new problems of administration facing the Manchus
and to gather able men around him. The most capable of
the surrendering Chinese were always placed in his service
and became his advisers.[40] When T'ai-tsung died, Dorgon
became regent for the third and still young Manchu emperor
and as such led the Manchu armies in 1644 into Peking and
to the conquest of China Proper. It was a Chinese adminis-

---

[39] The Chinese officials seem to have often emphasized this state philosophy. And the Manchus, somewhat angry over the poor Chinese participation
and heroism in battles, accused them of not holding these rules themselves.
Compare K. K. F. L., XXIV, pp. 451-2.

[40] K. K. F. L., Chapter XV, Hauer, p. 288.

trative policy that he had acquired in Manchuria and which he could apply to the whole of China after the conquest.[41]

Feudalism had given the Manchus their first integrating power. The acceptance of bureaucracy in the banner and central administration made them a state. It was the Chinese system, Chinese officials and Chinese ideas that enabled the Manchus to conquer China.

[41] Compare Dorgon's biography in Ch'in Ting Tsung Shih Wang Kung Kung Chi Piao ch'uan 欽定宗室王公功績表傳. Translated by Hauer in Ostas. Zeitschrift, Neue Folge, III. Heft 1, pp. 9 ff.

CHAPTER VII

THE CLAN ELEMENT IN THE MANCHU STATE

The Vassalage of the Mongol Tribes

Traditional history has dealt with the Mongol and Tungus tribal people as consisting of a number of clans. The clans, the enlarged exogamic family groups of agnati, with clan names, bound together by shamanistic clan spirits and common ancestor worship were supposed to be the economic and political units that formed the tribes.[1] This traditional interpretation can apparently no longer be upheld without modification, after new light has been thrown on the question by the analysis of Liao society by Wittfogel and Feng. This analysis shows that the word "clan" should not be injudiciously used.[2] Aside from the ruling families the Liao had no clans in the strict sense of the word. Their loose exogamic kinship groups had no clan names, were broken up and reformed after a few generations and did not form that "historical and magic unity" which the clan was supposed to be. Wittfogel avoids therefore the name "clan" and speaks instead of "kinship groups" or "lineages" to express the idea of certain loosely knitted temporary family units. On the whole he discovers a "clanless" tribal society with the peoples in Inner Asia in general. Only certain ruling groups—two in the case of the Liao—assume the shape of veritable clans, although they also have been formed "synthetically." Dealing with these with regard to their general social structure rather than their kinship components the term "clan" is applied to them "preliminarily and tentatively" by Wittfogel, although otherwise they are called "lineages."

Applying these results to the Manchu society it can be said

[1] Shirokogoroff, *Social Organization of the Manchus.*
[2] Wittfogel-Feng, *Liao,* section VII.

that the Manchu "clans" were in their formations also somewhat vague. The lower people had no clans of their own but
joined the group of leading nobles. For the noble families
there where, however, a number of clan names.[3] And the
imperial house "Aisin Kioro" had a clan history surrounded
with a number of legends. True, they were made up later
to give the family the necessary standing in Chinese eyes.
Ancestor worship was also started for political reasons.
But the effect remains the same; and, granting that the clan
structure of the Manchus was loose, not original and limited
to the upper groups, it still seems justifiable to apply the
term clan in these cases, as we are interested more with the
political structure than with the kinship problem.

Of course the size of such a clan group or the question
through how many generations it would hold together, would
depend on the economic and political feasibility. If the
group became too large it would break apart and a new
clan or new group would be formed with new symbols.
How large a kinship group could become before it was split
by division depended a great deal on outside circumstances.
Exhausted hunting grounds could result in a division of
hunters' groups, etc. Two kinds of political circumstances
would, however, tend to keep clans, although large, to
gether. Firstly, if a group was threatened by outside danger,
it would most likely remain united in its fight for survival.
And secondly, if a group ascended to political leadership and
became a political power, families that otherwise might have
split off would in this case hang on to share in the spoils
of victory. If a nomad group, therefore, succeeded in building up a successful frontier state, a large clan would be
leading the group. For the clan relationship was not broken
up by the development of feudalism. The fact that the members of the clans advanced from free hunters or nomads to
the position of the control over serfs and landed income

[3] The *Pa-ch'i Man-chou shih-tsu t'ung-p'u* （八旗滿洲氏族通譜）
comprehensive genealogy of the Manchu clans, printed in 1745, contains
such a list. I am indebted to Dr. Tang Chao-ying of the Congressional
Library in Washington with whom I had several discussions on the character
of Manchu clans.

did not destroy the bond of the clans. On the contrary clan unity strengthened all clan members, who profited by it likewise.

Not only the leading group upheld its clan bond, the other people also kept their clan associations, as far as they had formed clans before they joined the new state. As the clans had their own authority, a dualism of political control with the feudal and bureaucratic state authority resulted that could create difficulties. This dualism was of real importance only in the case of the leading clan, the clan of the ruler of the new state.

The clan authority was a rather democratic affair. Clan meetings, where the clan head—usually a representative of the senior line—presided, decided on clan affairs. With the growth of the political power of the state, the members of the leading clan would naturally endeavor to extend this "democratic" principle to the control of the whole state— in other words to share in the government. Monarchical and clan power were thus in competition with each other, with a number of inherent dangers for the political stability and unity of government.

The possible danger of disunity would become more evident with the second generation after the establishment of the state. In the first generation was the man who had created the power, who with his qualities of leadership and energy had led his group to success and victory. Naturally his authority as ruler over the state and even within the clan would be comparatively uncontested. The very fact that he emerged and gained control of a larger following was the condition and beginning of the clan's success.

But to gain his success this first ruler would have to depend on the help and cooperation of his clan, as it would take time to develop a political organization. When this first leader died, it would be difficult for his successor to assure himself against the personal ambition and rivalry of important men of the clan who had become entrenched in their positions during the first period. A struggle between the idea of monarchical power and that of clan autonomy or even among different persons for supremacy would often ensue and would lead to results disastrous for the state. Only if the ruler of a frontier state could assert himself against the clan could he organize a centralized power strong enough to survive or penetrate further into China. The problem of stability depended on the elimination of the clan members' political power by the ruler, because otherwise this power would inevitably lead to the breaking up of unity of the state as numerous examples of frontier history show.

One difficulty for the ruler in such struggles was the strength of the clan tradition. The ruler had to be careful and diplomatic in his dealings with the clan members. He could not act against the clan as such; he would have to single out certain persons and act against them with the consent of the rest of the clan. The elimination of clan influence was thus at best a slow process. Even if rebellions of clan members occurred and were put down, it was—as frontier history shows—sometimes impossible or at least difficult to eliminate the rebellious relatives, brothers, or others too nearly related to be harmed even after defeat.[4] Many former frontier dynasties in Chinese history had been greatly weakened or caused to fall by such internal conflicts.

The most critical period for possible conflicts arising from this situation was that following the death of a ruler. Division of power between important and influential clan members could lead to competition between rival candidates.[5] The

[4] In Liao history, in the beginning at least, rebellious brothers of the ruler had to be defeated several times with heavy losses for the Liao people on both sides without the leading brothers suffering at first bodily harm. The wife of one brother, however, coming from another kinship group and regarded also as the *spiritus rector* of the rebellion was hanged. Later such clemency disappeared. Compare Wittfogel-Feng, *Liao*, XIII, also Gabelentz, Liao translation, pp. 12-13.

[5] The possibility of fighting for the succession is of course a general danger for all regimes without a fixed order of succession. If the clan tradition made such fights possible, it also had a certain restraining effect. The clan also bound its members together by their common interests. This can be seen in comparison with the Ottoman state where many sons and possible successors were born in the harem of the ruler without any restraint of clan tradition as a check on their personal ambitions. To avoid fights between heirs, the Osmanlis therefore ruthlessly killed all of them except the successor, once this successor had been determined. Compare Toynbee, *op. cit.*, p. 33, note 1.

general tradition of succession in Manchu clan leadership was particularly unfortunate in this connection. It determined that the new ruler be chosen out of the men of the next generation, but by the men of the older generation.[6] Who actually had the say in such elections depended not only on personal influence, but more generally on the age of the two generations involved. The age relationship of the two generations depended again on the age the former ruler had reached. If this ruler had died young, his generation would still be in the active age, while the next generation had not come to influence. If the ruler grew old, his generation had in practice possibly already lost some of its influence to the younger generation. In any case there was much occasion for rivalries and jealousies that could become fatal to the group.

With the Manchus this danger never became so grave that it broke the restraining check of political institutions and of group unity. The Manchus were thus spared the worst aspect of divided rule and control. But there remained the problem of the elimination of clan influence and power in order to give the ruler the absolute authority needed for a lasting centralized bureaucratic government over Chinese territory and people.

Nuerhaci had brought his family into powerful positions, for he had naturally needed the support of the outstanding men of his clan. Yet he had, interestingly enough, sought the support chiefly of the younger generation where his traditional authority prevented any danger of rivalry. His sons and nephews and their descendants who received the titles of beiles and beises [7] came to share in the new power. The banners were organized, as has been said, on a bureaucratic basis. But the ruler's family as a privileged group was given control over them and also participation in the administration. At first four family members—three sons

---

[6] This general tradition was in the first Manchu succession after Nuerhaci's death changed by Nuerhaci's institution of the Hosoi Beile described below.

[7] The title beile has been described above, Beise was one grade lower. Later Chinese princely titles were introduced.

and one nephew—were chosen to control one banner each, at the time when there were only four banners. Three other sons and one grandson of Nuerhaci were chosen for a similar position when the other four banners were created. This control was given to them to remain hereditary in their families. Each of the men had gained this position at least partly on his own merits as companion in arms of the ruler. But it implied forthwith a tremendous power, as each was to control his banner's whole economy. This position necessarily gave the bearer an extraordinary standing in the council of the nation. The eight leaders thus created became known as the four senior and for junior beiles.[8] Not the whole clan, but eight outstanding members of the clan shared thus in the rule of the state. They gained their position as trusted junior members of the clan, but as their position was hereditary, they became in reality great feudal lords. Only the bond of the clan, the bond of the common interest of the group, could keep these nobles from misusing their position.

To eliminate or diminish the danger of feudal autonomy of these most important pillars of the Manchu state their position was made more formal and at the same time more pseudo-bureaucratic when they received in 1622 the title Hosoi Beiles.[9] This formal appointment to govern the eight banners as the "eight houses of the Hosoi Beile," as they came to be called, transformed clan power into an institution

[8] 四大貝勒, 四小貝勒. The four senior beiles were Daisan, Amin, Manggultai and Abahai, often named singly because of their importance. Compare *K. K. F. L.,* Chapters V, 68, IX etc.

[9] 和碩貝勒. *K. K. F. L.,* Chapter VII, p. 23. The word Hosoi itself has been explained in different ways. It is probably the genetive derived from a Manchu word Hoso meaning corner. Pelliot and Hauer following him translate it as "apanage," meaning that the Hosoi Beile were great apanaged princes. Haenisch states however that Hoso or Hosoi can in no dictionary and in no particular connection elsewhere be found with the meaning "apanage." He thinks it to be a Manchu translation of the Chinese word fang (方), corner, which appeared in the Chinese official title Fang Po (方伯) "count of the corner," of old origin and still used under the Ming for provincial treasurers. As a word of feudal origin but with later beaucratic meaning it would lend itself indeed to use as a title for the important Manchu leaders. If Haenisch's opinion is correct, it would be another instance of Chinese influence in the shaping of the new Manchu state. Compare Haenisch, "Hosoi Cin Wang," *Asia Major,* II, 590.

of the government. The Hosoi Beiles formed also the highest council of state. Nuerhaci had used high dignitaries before to help him with the growing administration. His government secretaries and executive secretaries, appointed in 1616, have been mentioned already. They were his technical advisers. In political questions, however, he had to rely, before his descendants grew up, on the help and advice of a few older companions in arms.[10] Now he found in the younger generation of his clan a group of men for this assistance. Already in 1621 he had started the practice of having the four senior Beiles take monthly turns as the administrative head of national affairs—a sort of temporary Prime Minister.[11] This practice was continued, and in addition the council of the Hosoi Beile was created. The clan was thus permitted to share in the ruling power. But at the same time the misuse of this power by individual members of the clan for their own ends was made difficult. The participation of the Hosoi Beiles in this council meant a check on their control of the individual banners. According to Nuerhaci's will the council should lead to an active participation of each in state affairs. Anyone who could not or would not take part in shaping the policy would lose his position, which another young clan member would receive instead. Nobody would be allowed to go on trips solely on his own responsibility and without informing the others. And, most important of all, " all questions shall not be discussed privately by one or two men, but commonly deliberated in a meeting of all. If a report is presented to the throne, all together have to appear for the report." [12]

The appointment of the Hosoi Beiles and their council transformed the clan element into a quasi-bureaucratic insti-

[10] *K. K. F. L.,* Chapter VII, p. 111, where Eidu and Fionggon were mentioned as old generals with the title "assistants in government." (車甫國政).

[11] *K. K. F. L.,* Chapter XII, p. 5.

[12] *K. K. F. L.,* Chapters VII and VIII, p. 1. This transformation of clan nobles into a quasi-bureaucratic institution did not go too smoothly, as the beiles had to be frequently admonished not to follow their own selfish interests, but to think of the common welfare. *K. K. F. L.,* Chapter VIII, p. 137, etc.

tution. Together with the "professional" officials and the dignitaries they formed the government of the ruler. Most of the ruler's edicts and statements were addressed to all of them. And in military campaigns the Hosoi Beiles shared the command with other deserving leaders.[13]

But the most important function of the Hosoi Beile was to begin only after Nuerhaci's death. According to Nuerhaci's wish they were to elect the successor to the throne.[14] And this they did.[15] They elected with little delay or difficulty Nuerhaci's eighth son, Abahai, as successor.

With this change of ruler, the position of the Hosoi Beile became automatically different and of much greater importance. When Nuerhaci had given the clan, through the institution of the Hosoi Beile, a great share in political control, he had himself nevertheless remained the uncontested and outstanding leader of the nation. The Beiles had been the assistants of the ruler but in no way his equals. They had to obey him not only as officials, but also as clan members, as he belonged to the older generation.

With Abahai, the new emperor, this was completely different. He was of the same generation as the Hosoi Beiles with one exception. He himself had been one of them. He was the fourth of the senior Beiles. The three other senior Beiles were furthermore of higher age. Although there was in Manchu life a recognized tendency toward inheritance by junior sons, the seniors nevertheless deserved a certain respect. For Abahai, therefore, the powerful position of the Hosoi Beiles in the banners and in the central government meant simply a limitation of his own power and control as ruler. The question of the clan power versus monarchical power became an issue. Nuerhaci had with his institution of

[13] Compare the campaign against Korea, which, however, is only one of many examples.

[14] K. K. F. L., Chapter VII, p. 116. By this regulation the general clan tradition was given up for the election of Nuerhaci's successor. (Compare note 4.) The Hosoi Beile were of the same generation or even younger than the successor. After Abahais' death it was again the older generation that decided the election.

[15] K. K. F. L., Chapter IX, p. 3.

the Hosoi Beile meant to give the clan through them a pre-
ponderant influence after his own death.

The ceremony of the inauguration of Abahai showed the
difference. It was really a clan affair. An oath was taken by
the clan members and the ruler in which they mutually
vowed each other loyalty.[16] " Brothers and brothers' sons "
was the term under which in both oaths the family community was named and mutual support was promised.
Abahai—or T'ai-tsung with his temple name—promised to
honor his elder brothers and elders and to love his younger
brothers and their sons and to follow the right way. The
clan oath ended with the words " if we are unanimously
one house and have no concealed and bad thoughts, Heaven
and Earth shall both give us benevolent help." [16]

The new emperor's first position as *primus inter pares* of
his clan rather than as an autocratic ruler could be recognized in several ways. The way he talked to his elder brothers
on their return from successful campaigns,[17] the way they
were seated at receptions at his right and left side instead
of below him,[18] indicated the respect he owed them. The
Beile Amin showed in his undisciplined actions how little
he cared about the emperors authority. Even in later years
the elder Beiles' voices had to be heard in military
campaigns.[19]

But slowly T'ai-tsung succeeded in wresting the power from
the hands of the clan and in particular from those of his elder
brothers and in building up his own authority. For this purpose the development of a bureaucracy, needed for so many
other reasons, was also a useful weapon. This development
served thus not only the general administrative needs of
the state, but also T'ai-tsung's personal aim to create a
monarchical rather than a clan government. The success of
his policy was decisive for the further greatness of the

[16] *K. K. F. L.,* Chapter IX, p. 5.
[17] *K. K. F. L.,* Chapter IX, p. 23.
[18] *K. K. F. L.,* Chapter X, p. 1.
[19] *K. K. F. L.,* Chapter XII, pp. 206-7, where the elder Beile disagree with
the Emperor and have to be persuaded; an incident that creates general
misgivings.

Manchu state, as the survival of the clan power would most likely have ultimately led to the same kind of inner cleavage with which former frontier states had to cope.

T'ai-tsung began his policy immediately after he came to the throne in 1626 with a reorganization of the banner administration. At that time two of the banners were under his own control, as he had not complied with Nuerhaci's last wish, that one vacant banner should be given to T'ai-tsung's brother, Ajiige.[20] T'ai-tsung kept this banner for himself in addition to his own banner. Aside from this he introduced for all the banners a larger staff of administrative officers. The authority for the banners remained for a while with the Hosoi Beiles. But the actual command and administration came more into the control of a staff of officers, of which the highest took part in all consultations with the ruler on banner affairs and other government business, led the march of their troops in campaigns and had to examine and hear all banner matters. The lower officers were divided into civil officials who decided the law cases and dealt with administration, and military officials who led their units in military training and campaigns.[21] Thus the position of the Hosoi Beile was weakened at the very source of their power, while the bureaucratization of the banners went one step further.

Another step was taken by T'ai-tsung in 1629, when the three remaining senior Beiles were deprived of their position as head of the administration, which they had held in monthly rotation since Nuerhaci's time. Under the pretext that the elder brothers should not alone be troubled with this work, the younger brothers and nephews were ordered by T'ai-tsung to take the job instead, sharing it between themselves in monthly turns.[22] With the handing over of this post from the seniors to the juniors, T'ai-tsungs authority must have been strengthened.

After this, T'ai-tsung began to get rid of these superior

[20] See Abahai's biography in A. W. Hummel, *Eminent Chinese of the Ch'ing Period.*
[21] *K. K. F. L.,* Chapter IX.   [22] *K. K. F. L.,* Chapter XII, p. 5.

elders altogether. Of the three, Amin, T'ai-tsung's cousin, soon gave cause for discontent. His disregard of the emperors orders in the Korean campaign has already been described. Amin had then not succeeded in looting the Korean capital as he had hoped. But he had done nevertheless a bit of looting of his own and made his special treaty with the king of Korea. At that time T'ai-tsung did not apparently feel strong enough to act. He received Amin on the return from this campaign with all honors. But three years later, in 1630, Amin, then in command of the rear guard of the Manchu army in a campaign in China, misbehaved again. After a brutal and entirely unnecessary slaughter of the civilian population, he deserted his own troops, who suffered heavy losses in their retreat. Weakened in power, he was on his return put into prison where he died 10 years later. His banner was given to his brother Jirgalang. T'ai-tsung had got rid of the most violent of the senior Hosoi Beile.[23]

Two years later, in 1632, the two remaining elder Hosoi Beile, Daisan and Manggultai gave up their seats at each side of the emperor at receptions. The pretext was some misbehavior of Manggultai.[24] The two elder Beile were in future to sit flanking the approach to the emperor's chair. With this new seating order disappeared the last outer sign of a limitation of T'ai-tsung power by elder or other clan members. A year before, in 1631, the six ministries had been introduced, a step by which the whole administration was put on a bureaucratic basis by the emperor, who controlled it. Manggultai was, after his death in 1633, posthumously accused of treason and his banner was taken from the control of his family and placed under the direct control of T'ai-tsung, who thus had direct control over three of the eight banners.[25] T'ai-tsung thus succeeded without any real opposition in asserting himself as a monarch and in ridding himself of the major restrictions of the clan element.

[23] *K. K. F. L.*, Chapter XIII, Hauer, *K. K. F. L.*, p. 240.
[24] *K. K. F. L.*, Chapter XV, Hauer, *K. K. F. L.*, p. 290.
[25] A differentiation between the three " superior " banners and the five " inferior " banners was thus introduced.

When T'sai-tsung died in 1643, the clan regained importance. T'ai-tsung's efforts had weakened the clan influence in government, but had not resulted in creating any other council for the highest state decisions that were at the same time clan affairs, such as the succession. The Hosoi Beile had lost their position in favor of the bureaucratic ministries. But no arrangement had been made for the nomination of the successor. As a result, the discussion after T'ai-tsung's death involved a large group of leading clan members and officials and led to a conflict of opinion that was overcome only after 17 days of debate, and not without leaving some misgivings.[26]

The strong man of the time was prince Dorgon. It has been described before how Dorgon as head of the ministry of the interior had been appointed to the most important and decisive post in the new bureaucratic administration. As actual organizer and creator of the new bureaucracy he became the exponent and champion of the new form of government. As such he would have to carry the brunt of the clan animosity against limitation of clan power in favor of the monarchical idea. As Dorgon was rather self-willed and not free of personal ambition, this animosity became rather bitter and led after his death to the deprivation of all his former titles and rank and the degradation of his memory. Only later Manchu history rehabilitated him.[27]

Prince Dorgon was the fourteenth son of Nuerhaci and the younger brother of the second Manchu ruler T'ai-tsung or Abahai. Under his brother's rule Dorgon had revealed himself to be not only an excellent organizer and administrator but also an extremely gifted military leader.[28] When

[26] See Gibert, op. cit., also Hauer, "Prince Dorgon," see note 7.
[27] The very interesting life of Prince Dorgon can be found in Ch'in ting tsung shih wang kung kung chi piao chuan, 欽定宗室王公功績表傳, translated by E. Hauer in Ostasiatische Zeitschrift, Neue Folge III, Heft 1. The following details were taken from this biography.
[28] His title, Jui, Manch. Mergen, means clever, indicating that he gained his military fame more by strategy than being a dare-devil. Yet he did not avoid personal danger, so that once his entourage was blamed for not taking better care for his protection against risks. He was rather self-willed and of independent judgement. Once Dorgon disobeyed, probably for good reasons,

Dorgon's brother, the emperor T'ai-tsung died, Dorgon because of his talent and training would have been the man
to take over the rulership himself. But as he was of the
same and not the next generation, he could not, according
to clan tradition, become emperor himself. There was nevertheless a conspiracy in his favor, which he, however, revealed to the clan, so that the conspirators received capital
punishment. He accepted the election of the emperor Shun-
Chih, the twelfth son of T'ai-tsung, a five year old child,
while he himself and Jirgalang his cousin Hosoi Beile and
head of another clan faction, became co-regents and shared
the actual power.

This was a compromise solution. It revealed the fact
that none of the leaders of the older generation, including
Dorgon himself, were willing to renounce their own power.
Therefore a young child was put on the throne with no voice
yet of its own. Haoge, the eldest son of T'ai-tsung and
already a grown up man, had been another candidate. But—
in Dorgon's words—"the princes and high dignitaries all
said: ' If the Su Ch'in wang (Hagoe) is placed on the throne
we all shall have no standing.' "

Of the two new regents, Dorgon was the real power. He
set to work to weaken the clan influence and particularly to
destroy the power of his antagonists in the clan. Even if he
was not free of personal ambition, his policy resulted chiefly
in the strengthening of the central bureaucratical power of
the state and the emperor.

Shortly after Dorgon's appointment as regent he decreed
that the control of the princes, beiles and beises, (in other
words of the clan nobility) over the six ministries should
end. He also gained preeminence over his co-regent Jirgalang. The latter instructed the dignitaries of the court and
ministries to report government affairs first to Dorgon and
to place his name first on documents. All this happened in
the same year, 1644, in which Dorgon led the Manchus
to Peking, placed the boy emperor on the dragon throne and

military orders of his ruling brother. He was punished with the loss of one
unit of his warrior serfs. Dorgon accepted this punishment without grudge.

established the Manchu power over China. The military and diplomatic skill displayed by him in this successful undertaking was amazing and served, of course, to strengthen his position in the state.

In the coming years he built up the Manchu power over China. He strengthened further the power of bureaucratic institutions; and it was not in contradiction with this policy if he at the same time undertook the elimination of his opponents in the clan. Personal ambition and state policy went well together in his case. In 1647 Dorgon succeeded in getting rid of the Co-regent Jirgalang, who was deposed " because while building his palace he had tresspassed the rules and had used bronze lions, turtles and cranes without being entitled to them." A further degradation of Jirgalang came later on the accusation that he had, in 1644, privately conspired to make Haoge emperor and that he had omitted to promote officials in the imperial yellow banners, while on the other hand the blue banners of his faction had been permitted to take the front positions when the Manchus had entered Peking. These trifling accusations were of course only pretexts and show simply a clan rivalry which Jirgalang never forgot and which made him after Dorgon's death the leader of the group that demanded Dorgon's posthumous degradation.

In Jirgalang's place Dorgon chose his own younger brother Dodo as co-regent, but this was in fact not more than a nominal limitation of his own power. In the year 1647 Dorgon also got rid of his former rival candidate, Haoge, who was imprisoned and was said to have been poisoned. The fact that Dorgon took Haoge's former wife into his own house did not make this story any better.

These and other acts of personal arbitrariness resulted in overshadowing for some time the fame of this perhaps greatest of the Manchu leaders. He had been responsible not only for the march on Peking but also for a policy that immediately accepted and confirmed the majority of local Chinese officials in their positions, preventing a chaos that would have allowed a stronger Ming opposition. He honored and buried the Ming emperor slaughtered by the bandits and thus gave his authority an appearance of Chinese legality. But he also abolished immediately all extra taxation that had been the cause of unrest and rebellion. He thus accepted and strengthened the bureaucratic administration found in China, and he did not permit the Manchu imperial clan to interfere with this administration. In 1649 he warned the Chinese officials against permitting such interference: "If princes or palace dignitaries interfere in goverment affairs of the ministries or in the promotion or degradation of Chinese officials in the capital or in the provinces, they will be punished without further ado and regardless of whether they were right or wrong. If promotions of officials become necessary I shall promote, and if degradations are necessary I shall degrade. Should we perhaps, like at the end of the Ming, listen partially to the words of third persons or promote and degrade wantonly? Regarding summons by princes into their palaces of officials not under their orders, the fault is with the princes. If the officials obey the summons, the fault is with the officials. If summons should become necessary, the princes must first report to the throne and get permission."

Dorgon thus established the authority of the throne and prevented the development of powerful rival clan leaders. If he served at the same time his own ambition for power as the regent and if he assumed certain tokens and characteristics of imperial position such as robes, a greater number of bodyguards, palaces, etc., there is no proof that he aspired for more and hoped to gain the throne for himself, as his enemies said after his death. On the contrary his actions against attempts of others to place him on the throne indicate that he was a loyal supporter not only of the monarchical idea, but also of the existing monarch and the order of succession. If he was jealous of his position as regent, he was certainly the best qualified man for this position, and his efforts really completed the work of the foundation of the Manchu dynasty that had been begun by Nuerhaci.

The final elimination of the power of the imperial clan

came only later under the emperor K'ang-hsi, when the imperial clansmen became excluded from any administrative office of high political importance. The institutions of government, once established to replace clan and feudal control, were then even cleared of the persons that belonged to the clan. And these persons were deprived of all but the enjoyment of a privileged social position with a great income. And from the past there did not survive much more than the distinction of the girdle, yellow or red according to the nearness of relationship to the emperor, which Nuerhaci had allowed the members of the imperial clan to wear, and a sizable income for the members of the imperial family. It was the completion of a long development of struggle against the clan power, a struggle of which the outcome in favor of the monarchical order was decisive for the Manchu success.

There was, of course, in the Manchu social structure, not only the imperial clan. A number of other clans are known, but only the imperial clan, the clan of the ruling group, was of great political importance and a real problem. For the rest the clans survived as social institutions without however greatly affecting the new organization of the state. The clan heads—Mokunda—still held their positions, which were indirectly connected with the banner to which the clan belonged. The company commanders of the banners received recruiting lists from the Mokunda. In clan affairs the Mokunda was even the higher authority. Officers, as members of the clan, had to obey the Mokunda's orders in clan affairs, had to come to clan meetings, and could be punished if they did not. All orders and regulations of military authorities were announced for the knowledge of the clan members through the Mokunda. There was thus cooperation between military organization and the clans.[29]

In civil affairs, the Mokunda was held responsible in cases concerning clan members. Only in very serious cases did the authorities act directly. The Mokunda had limited jurisdiction inside the clan. The interclan relations, on the other

[29] Shirokogoroff, *Social Organization of the Manchus,* pp. 53, 55.

hand, were taken over by the state. The clan element thus remained together with feudalism and bureaucracy a part of the Manchu state's social organization.

* * *

During the process of building their state, the Manchus greatly changed their society and political life. From forest tribes, they changed to feudal lords and bureaucrats and accepted Chinese political organizations and ideologies, integrating them with their own. Various elements were thus integrated to a new growth on a preeminently Chinese basis. Yet not everything included by the Manchus in their state, was integrated to the same degree into this organization. The Mongols became a part of the Manchu state, but their world remained far less affected by social and political development. The Chinese life transformed the Manchus, and the frontier could also be transformed in its life. But the conditions beyond could not be changed for those people who remained in the steppes. The tribal society of the Mongols did join the Manchus but remained for the most part unchanged. The Mongols became allies under Manchu control rather than an integral part of the new state organization. Some resisting tribes were broken up, destroyed and the remainders included into the Manchu banners.[30] Some other tribes had by themselves moved into the frontier region and changed their society.[31] But the steppe society as such could hardly be changed.

This steppe society has been described in different ways. It has usually been called feudal. If this word is to be used, one has to keep in mind that it would have one meaning with the Manchus as described above, and another meaning when applied to the Mongols. The Mongol nobles of the

[30] *I. e.,* the Chahars and Tumets.

[31] Thus the Easternmost Mongols, who were also not conquered by the Manchus but had rather " allied " themselves after defeat, had already a certain amount of agriculture, carried on for them by Chinese tenants. The Khitan with their economy of cattle breeding in Jehol had also developed some agriculture there (see Wittfogel-Feng, *Liao,* section II). Compare also the mixed Mongol.-Manchu-Chinese composition of the Yehe state.

steppe aristocracy had serfs, but without agriculture they lacked the strict attachment of one noble household to a definite piece of land, the distinguishing characteristic of true feudalism. Without this connection with the land, the status of the serf or dependent man could be "freer" than with agrarian feudalism. With the latter the man meant for the lord nothing but his labor. If he wanted to run away, he could not take the land with him. But the property in the steppe was movable cattle. And the man with cattle was worth more to his lord and to others. The power of one lord therefore never became as exclusive, as if it would have become had it been based on territory, and the strength of the groups or the clans were proportionally greater.

There was also in the steppe a certain attachment to the land; the mobility was not unlimited; summer and winter pastures made up a definite territory for each group; but it was the whole group, not the single lord, to which this territory belonged. The Mongol society will therefore here be called tribal rather than feudal, following a distinction proposed by Owen Lattimore.

The Manchus could not change much this tribal social structure of the Mongols. They could only follow the Chinese example and rule the Mongols through the latter's spiritual and secular leaders. It was a vassal relationship, such as the outer regions always had had to the Chinese dynasty. It contained, however, for the Manchus the same dangers of attack from beyond the frontier as the Chinese had had to face, the danger of agglomeration of power under one leading clan. To avoid it the Manchus applied to the Mongols the same policy of *divide et impera* that had been applied by the Chinese Ming to the Mongols and the Manchus. They fixed the boundary for each Mongol tribe more rigidly than it had been done before, increasing the territorial limitation of mobility.[32] They gave the hereditary princes the sanction of imperial appointment and limited their power and the power of their families by the introduction of more

[32] *Ta Ch'ing Hui Tien, Li Fan Yuan* contains the lists of tribes, their boundaries, the chiefs and their positions.

bureaucratic leagues, whose heads could only be appointed by the emperor. They thus kept apart a number of tribal leaders. These leaders, the ruling Mongol class, were bound by a vassal relationship to the Manchu court.

This vassalage had a double importance. Firstly, it allowed the Manchu court a control and voice in Mongol affairs, so that even official imperial representatives could be placed at several major places in Mongol country as residents and political agents.[33] But during the rise of the Manchus these vassalages had a second, primarily strategic, importance for the Manchu campaigns in China. Not only were the Manchus assured against flank attacks by the Mongols, but they had in the Mongols auxiliary troops of considerable value. The Manchu army thus consisted not only of bureaucratic banners but also of feudal or tribal auxiliary troops. The necessity of keeping this heterogeneous army together under one discipline caused the Manchus to announce for this army before a campaign certain " instructions for the army in the field." [34] These disciplinary rules, stating how to behave against the enemy soldiers and people in conquerred territory, were not always simply decreed; they were sometimes sworn to by the whole army with a " yueh " (約), a compact, here of feudal character. The Mongols and their army thus formed a feudal-tribal annex to the Manchu state.

The state with which the Manchus conquered China, was formed on a bureaucratic Chinese basis with certain feudal characteristics and clan cohesion integrated into it, and a tribal Mongol vassal annex. It was based on a military banner organization copied from China but with feudal fragments and was ruled by the Manchu imperial clan and the emperor.

---

[33] The so-called Amban. Under the Manchu emperor Ch'ien-lung in the eighteenth century this control found its greatest extension.
[34] K. K. F. L., Chapter XII, Hauer, K. K. F. L., pp. 201, 207, 211; XVI, pp. 296, 300; XVIII, p. 345 etc.; XXXII, p. 584 etc.

CHAPTER VIII

THE MANCHUS AND THE CHINESE EMPIRE

We have discussed the several elements out of which the Manchus formed their political organization. The bureaucracy of China and the feudalism and clanism of the frontier and beyond became interacting and counteracting forces that integrated themselves into the Manchu state. It is, of course, only in theory that one can view them apart. In reality they formed a whole. They were, in their interaction, the forces that constituted the larger Chinese state system of China Proper and the outlying regions. The Manchu state was growing in the Chinese world at the edge of the Chinese empire. Its development can only be understood in its relationship to the Chinese empire, as it was—though a conquering force—still a part of China all the time.

At first the Chienchow guard and its head had owed a vassal allegiance to the Chinese emperor. From the view point of Chinese state philosophy there could be only one emperor,[1] set over all the earth, over people and vassals. The fact that the Manchus enlarged their original feudal territory and conquered more and more of Chinese Manchuria, would therefore not change the position of the Chinese emperor as head of the world state and representative of the heavenly will. But it would upset the "inner" arrangement and cut the bond between the emperor and the rebellious vassal. The emperor would have to use force to put the vassal in his place. This use of force was, according to the Chinese conception, not war of wars but punitive campaigns against rebellion. The Ming attempted such campaigns against the Manchus. But all their attempts to crush the growing Manchu power, first by an offensive into Manchu

---

[1] The Chinese explanation by natural phenomena can therefore be said to be that: there can be only one emperor on earth as there is only one sun in heaven.

territory or later simply by seeking to stem the Manchu tide by defense, failed.

There would of course have been also the possibility of " appeasement." The reestablishment of peace and order in the empire meant not of necessity a return to the *status quo ante*. The recognition of the Manchu conquests and the acceptance of the Manchus as a larger and more powerful frontier state within the empire would have been in theory quite possible. Indeed the Manchu rulers made a number of attempts to come to terms with the Chinese. There were periods of truce and of intercourse between the Chinese officials of the frontier and the Manchus. But there was never a settlement or peace. The formidable military state of the Manchus with its miniature imitation of Chinese state organization was too dangerous a competitor for world rulership to live with peacefully. The Chinese demanded the lost territory back. And the Manchus refused this demand, as they saw in the new land their most valuable possession.[2]

From the Chinese emperor's side there was thus a vacuum in the relationship with the Manchus. In a letter of the Ming emperor to Chinese frontier officials the statement was made that the Manchus were originally dependent;[3] but their present status remained open. They were simply rebels.

From the Manchu side the idea of vassalage was not given up for long. Nuerhaci had started out as the vassal of the Chinese emperor. And after the wars with the Ming had started, he and his successor did not give up the fiction for quite a time. Only at the very end of the struggle, when in 1636 the title of the Manchu ruling house was changed from Hou Chin to Ta Ch'ing did the struggle with the Ming become for the Manchus openly one between two equals.[4]

[2] 1627. *K. K . F. L.*, Chapter X, pp. 164, 166.

[3] 滿洲原係我屬國.

[4] It must be remembered that the Chin had never been rulers over all China. Of course, the tenor of the Manchu communications to the Chinese court and officials did show all during the periods of fighting and truce a strong arrogance. Compare the exchange of letters 1627, *K, K. F. L.*, X, but in these letters the Ming dynastical name was placed highest, indicating recognition of Ming suzerainty.

This veiled situation for the preceding time was possible as the vassalage of the Manchu ruler to the Chinese emperor did not—at least for the Manchus—exclude the possibility of fighting. The vassalage relationship, the "Meng" (盟) which had been sworn to locally by the Manchus and the Chinese frontier officials could be violated by either side. It has been disputed whether under the ancient Chinese feudal system the vassalage based on the Meng could be regarded as a two sided legal act, a contract.[5] The feudal frontier chiefs like the Manchus certainly regarded their vassalage as a two sided contract with obligations for the Chinese emperor, their suzerain, as well as for themselves. Violations of these obligations on the side of the emperor by his officials, were taken as a pretext to justify the Manchu war or feud with the Ming. The justification was given in the "seven great complaints" listed by Nuerhaci before the first attack on Fushun and repeated later as often as was thought necessary.[6] The seven great complaints were really a feudal declaration of war. They were directed against alleged violations of the overlord vassal relationship by the emperor's officials.

In many utterances of the Manchus this overlordship of the Chinese emperor remained recognized in theory. "The words of the emperor can, of course, not be opposed" said Nuerhaci during early negotiations with a Chinese frontier official about possession of fields on the frontier which he refused to give up, threatening the emperor with the possible nuisance value of his little country if not satisfactorily

[5] O. Franke, "Zur Beurteilung des chinesischen Lehenswesens," believes that there existed only a one-sided obligation on the side of the vassal prince.

[6] *K. K. F. L.*, Chapters V, p. 64; X, pp. 156, 162, etc. The seven great complaints were:
1. Violation of frontier and murder of Nuerhacis' father and grandfather.
2. Assistance given the Yehe.
3. Arrest of envoys, freed only after extradition of ten men, killed by the Ming on the frontier.
4. Assistance in marrying a Yehe girl, engaged to Nuerhaci, to a Mongol.
5. Ming soldiers prevent Manchus from harvesting contested fields.
6. Threatening letter in support of the Yehe.
7. Prevention of the incorporation of the Hada in the Manchu state and general assistance to the Yehe.

treated.[7] Later he claimed on several occasions that the position given by heaven to the ruler of the great country (China) imposed an obligation to fairness in the rule of the world.[8] The lack of this fair treatment and of neutrality of attitude in border strifes was the chief tenor of the seven complaints. Nuerhaci promised nevertheless several times to be obedient to the " great country," if he should only be recognized in his standing, that is, as being superior to the Chahar Mongols, who were then his enemies.[9] But he refused to return any of the territory he had conquered, advancing the argument that it belonged anyhow to the emperor as suzerain.[10] As this was said at the time of the first Manchu invasions into China Proper, it was a rather ironical recognition of the emperor's overlordship. Yet the idea expressed was in tune with the Chinese state conception.

The letters in which such statements were made did not reach the Ming emperor or come from him. It was a correspondence between the Manchu ruler and Chinese frontier officials. In the beginning the Manchu power had been too unimportant to be honored with direct communication with the emperor, except of course for the tribute missions to the court in Peking at regular intervals.[11] These ceased, however, with the fighting. And the court, unwilling to make any concessions to the dangerous frontier vassal, thought it beneath the dignity of the emperor to answer in person the rebel Manchu ruler. It was a constant complaint of the latter that he did not have direct contact with the emperor. His attempts to overcome the official barrier and his remarks on the question indicate that he felt realy offended. Once he succeeded in capturing the letter from the Ming emperor to frontier officials and in an attempted reply he did not deny his dependence.

This fiction of the Manchu state as a vassal of the Chinese

[7] *K. K. F. L.*, Chapter IV, p. 51. (帝之言自不可違.)
[8] 天建大國之君郎爲天下共主.
[9] 自當遜爾大國爾等志當視我居察命爾之上也.
[10] 且當天下之地盡爲爾朝廷所屬.
[11] See Chapter IV.

empire was given up only after 1636, when the Manchus set up a new dynasty under the name of Ta Ch'ing. The former title Hou Chin, taken in preparation for the first attack on the Chinese basin, had meant more the establishment of a feudal state than a claim to the rulership of the world, which "the" emperor was supposed to have, as the Chin had, in their period, only ruled North China. Until 1636 the Manchu policy was still disguised. The "Ta Yeh,"—the great realm—which was spoken of so often by Nuerhaci and his successor as something to be established could mean a feudal state and could mean more. With growing power the concealed reservation of gaining the Chinese throne—if possible—may have come to Nuerhaci comparatively early. But only after 1636 did the policy and intention become unmistakable and quite open. The change in attitude can be clearly seen in the relationship with Korea.

It has been related before how the king of Korea had been brought early to submission in order to secure the flank of the Manchus. He had become a Manchu vassal. But the Ming still remained for Korea, as a matter of course, the highest authority in the hierarchy. In 1636, however, after the change of the Manchu dynastic title and the new claim to world rulership, Korea was again informed. The king of Korea was asked to give up the year designation of the Ming and to accept the Manchu calendar instead. The king of Korea, fearing Ming vengeance, was afraid to take this step, and had to be forced by a new Manchu campaign to hand over the seal he had received from the Ming emperor and thus to break his former loyalty.[12] From a feudal ruler the Manchu chief had advanced to the claim of being the head of the Chinese system, the emperor of the world.

That meant that the Manchus had accepted the idea of the Chinese world state, and wanted to use it to further their own political ambitions. Indeed they had started out with the Chinese conception of the known world, as they had been from the beginning a part of it. The more they penetrated

[12] K. K. F. L., Chapter XXI, p. 398, and XXIII.

into Chinese territory and the more bureaucratic administration they had to introduce, the more Confucian ideology can also be found in the statements of their rulers. Erich Hauer has remarked that already the first two Manchu rulers, Nuerhaci or T'ai-tsu and his son and successor T'ai-tsung speak "like Confucian Sages." He sees in this the beginnig of a development which led to the disappearance of Manchu culture and their submergence in the "higher Chinese culture." [13] This statement is wrong both with regard to the Manchu background and with regard to the result of the development. Seen from the viewpoint of general political philosophy, Confucianism was the only possible state conception the Manchus could develop. There was no Manchu political world. The Chinese state was the known world state of their time and Confucianism the recognized state philosophy far beyond the borders of China proper. The Manchus built up their state at the edge and inside the cultural, economic and even the political frontiers of China. They used chiefly an economic system of organization. The adoption of the Chinese conception of the state was essential.

Thus the Manchu rulers referred to the model period and emperors of Chinese antiquity to create an ideology justifying their own attitude. They spoke of the favor of heaven, which has no "private interests," [14] of the virtues of the emperor; of the people being his children whom he has to save from water and fire and of many other metaphors taken from Chinese political ideology. The people were supposed to flock to the Manchu state because of the virtues and care of the Manchu ruler. And his virtue finally enabled the emperor to receive and hold the mandate of heaven, to extend his sway over t'ien-hsia, the earth. All this was expressed in Chinese Confucian thought and wording. The Manchus introduced also the Chinese state and ancestor cult. And to make this state philosophy the common knowledge of their young political leaders, the Manchu rulers promoted

[13] E. Hauer, introduction to translation of *K. K. F. L.*
[14] *K. K. F. L.*, Chapter V, p. 2.

the translation and reading of countless Chinese Confucian books, and the education of the young Manchus in their ideas. The Chinese had based the education of their officials on the knowledge of the writings of the ancient philosophers. They had thus created the scholar-gentry class. The Manchus were on the way to follow suit.

This application of Chinese philosophy, the talk about virtue and Tao, the principle of harmony with nature, even the fiction of the suzerainty of the Chinese emperor sustained through the time of the fight against him, must seem at first view pretty much like a farce if one compares all this with the reality of a very ambitious and carefully planned scheme of expansion and military conquest. Yet one must not forget that behind the philosophical language of Chinese states ethics there were always hidden very real political processes. It was always but an idealization of reality. And when the Manchus used these terms and language, it simply showed their realization and acceptance of Chinese political realities. While building up a Chinese administration, the Manchus needed the Chinese ideology.

But if the Manchus found it necessary to accept Chinese phraseology and ideology as justification for their political life, they did not accept everything that had the nimbus of Chinese antiquity. T'ai-tsung stated: "In the chronicles of Chinese literature there are many beautiful words which are useless even after detailed study." And he ordered his officials to choose from the histories of the Sung, the Liao, the Chin and the Yuan dynasties those sections for collection and translation, which portrayed the country as flourishing through diligent work aimed at a well ordered government and as declining in opposite circumstances or set forth the deeds of military leaders and the influences of clever men and scoundrels, of loyal servants and flatterers, on the interests of the state.[15] Even the Chinese phraseology itself was indeed in Manchu minds and mouths something different. They were warriors and behind many of their Chinese quotations one can sense an attitude which did not

[15] *K. K. F. L.*, Chapter XX, p. 9.

agree with the original meaning. Virtue was not the mature following of the Tao, the path of nature, in the terms of Mencius; it was not the winning of others by example. It was a very military virtue. When once the Chinese complained about their heavy burden and unfair treatment in comparison with the Manchu nobility, they were told that the Manchus had earned this position through their merits in the war. They did the fighting, they ran the risks. And a rather martial interpretation was thus given to the philosopher's words: "If the head of the family can maintain the worthy man, he will obtain a Kuo; and if the prince of a Kuo can maintain the worthy men, then he will obtain the rulership of the earth." [16] Not the sages or philosophers, but the warriors were the worthy men for the Manchus.

The Manchu rulers also claimed to have the Tao or heaven's support. They believed that it was necessary for a ruler to have it. But when they compared their own virtue and "goodness" with the virtue—and Taoless Chinese emperor we realize that this Tao was nothing but a political slogan. The excuse for the attack on the Chahar Khan was that "he has no Tao." [17] And the military meaning of this Tao becomes clear when they professed: "Whoever has it, has military success, who does not have it, fails in the field." [18] It was perhaps more honest when T'ai-tsung said on the occasion of his proclamation as emperor: ". . . by keeping peace inside and grabbing outside a great empire is rising . . . ." [19] The Manchus using Chinese state philosophy were thus certainly not true disciples of Mencius.

As has been seen, the Chinese bureaucratic administration and the Chinese "children subjects" were only a part of the original Manchu state. There was another, feudal, frontier half of it, also with its own tradition. The Manchus fell

---

[16] 有家者能養賢，則取國而可得。有國者能養賢則取天下而天下可得。 K. K. F. L., Chapter XVIII, pp. 5 ff. Compare also Chapter V, p. 55.

[17] K. K. F. L., Chapter XXIV, p. 4.

[18] 蓋聞古來用兵征代。有道者昌。無道者廢.

[19] K. K. F. L., XXI, p. 15.

heirs to his feudal militaristic thought which had been shaped in their own society. From the Liao and Chin history the Manchus knew the importance of military strength in gaining and later in keeping the throne. They had before their eyes the warning example of those other frontier peoples who had been spoiled by the comfortable life in China and thus had been defeated. They did not want to become " assimilated." But what they feared was not the dangerous influence of political theory or political organization. It was the danger for the physical strength of the race. The Manchu writing was created under T'ai-tsung's remarkable direction; it served to translate quantities of Chinese literature and philosophy into the national language, but among them also the histories of the Liao, Chin and Yuan. And T'ai-tsung, shortly after he accepted the new dynastic name admonished his Manchurian nobility never to forget the old art of mounted archery. It was a memorable scene when he gathered his princes, beiles and Manchu dignitaries around him and ordered a notable to read to the assembly from the history of the Chin, the kin of the Manchus. What was read was the edict of the Chin emperor Shih-tsung who warned his people not to imitate Chinese names and manners, to conserve the old straightness and simplicity and not to become extravagant and luxurious. After the reading T'ai-tsung spoke of the warning example of the history of the Chin, who did not heed their emperor's advice. They gave up mounted archery for wine and women, and their empire was destroyed. T'ai-tsung demonstrated that in Chinese dress the Manchus could not fight; yet, their fate depended on their military qualities.[20]

The Manchus thus felt themselves a part of the Chinese empire. Not only their organization but their ideology was of this Chinese empire. But as they came from the outer sphere of this empire, their ideology had a particular feudal frontier aspect in addition to the traditional Chinese thought. In

[20] *Tung Hua Lu* 6, pp. 18-19. For text of the Chin edict see Wieger, *textes historiques*, II, 1635.

this sense a dynasty that originated at the frontier was different from a dynasty originating in China proper.

There was still another difference between the two kinds of dynasties in the whole state-founding process. When a dynasty in China had "lost the heavenly mandate," it was not the same thing whether a rebel of inner China, a man from the people, founded a new dynasty, or whether a frontier ruler took over. In the first case there was no interposition, no half way. The founder of the Chinese Ming dynasty had not first established his own state. Li Tse-cheng, the rebel, who caused the downfall of the Ming and attempted to become emperor himself, could only be emperor or robber. The ministries and titles he created had never existed in law when he failed. The Chinese conception did not allow any intermediary state between a bandit and a successful usurper founding a new legal order.

This was different with a feudal frontier state such as the Manchus had established. At the frontier such feudal states were not only permitted but were the rule. Nuerhaci laid first a foundation (基) for a feudal state, a Kuo. He planned a Ta Yeh, a great state. The slow laborious process from the foundation upward has been frequently emphasized. At the beginning Nuerhaci did not even aim further than the establishment of a frontier state.[21] But the " state in the state " could be a preparation for the conquest of the larger Chinese state and was in this way an advantage for the frontier ruler over his Chinese rival in the competition for a vacant throne.

---

[21] Even the historiographs of the *K. K. F. L.* who wrote under order of the emperor Ch'ien-Lung over a hundred years after the establishment of the dynasty had to recognize this fact. See epilogue of Chapter I, *K. K. F. L.*

CHAPTER IX

CONCLUSION

In the development of the Manchu state organization as outlined in the preceding chapters can be seen an example of Chinese frontier history. The frontier always played an important part in Chinese history. Chinese control over outlying regions or outside penetration into Chinese agricultural country made this frontier alive. A zone was created through which outgrowing and ingrowing developments alternated in the course of time. These developments formed the background for Chinese expansion or barbarian invasion, which were both not simple military affairs, but complicated processes of transition.

Such an ingrowing process was the formation of the Manchu power. The conditions of the frontier region had prepared their start. It had been preceded by a military bureaucratic organization of the frontier by the Chinese Ming dynasty. The organization of the " Wei " by the Ming was an expansive Chinese move that was not only followed by the countermove of Manchu penetration but created a particularly favorable condition for this countermove. While former invading barbarians had to labor with the dualism of their own feudalism and the necessary bureaucracy in Chinese territory, the Manchus found in the Ming "Wei" a model organization that could be imitated for Manchu purposes and prevented the dualism for the Manchus.

On this model the Manchus built their banner organization. They created a state on a military bureaucratic basis, a state that grew in size, importance and institutional organization. This growth has been studied here in its elements. The transition from nomadism through feudalism to a bureaucratic state has been described with particular emphasis on the Chinese influence in the new edifice which the Manchus erected. The transition led to an interesting mixture

109

of political systems. An attempt has been made to describe one by one the various elements shaping the Manchu state. This dissection of a conglomerate body seemed necessary in order to point out the elements that with different emphasis at different times gave the Manchu state its form. Yet, one must not forget that the creation of the Manchu organization was a whole and indivisable process, a process of unification, adjustment and balancing that demanded no little statesmanship from its conceivers and originators.

The process began in the Ju-chen-Manchu region with a growing feudal power that swallowed its neighbors one by one. The first bureaucratic organization, the banner, was modeled after the Chinese Wei, on the other side of the border. But soon this border disappeared, the Chinese basin was invaded and became the new basis of the Manchus state. Chinese officials entered the state and the bureaucratic element of the frontier variety became the determining factor. The feudal element, although it never disappeared, lost in importance. The official position won the first place over the feudal income.

The other element of major importance was the position of the imperial clan. Clan power has always been of importance and often dangerous for the stability of states in frontier history. With Nuerhaci's ascendancy his clan had also been swept into power. After Nuerhaci's death the clan emerged more prominent and powerful, until the clan influence was slowly eliminated again in favor of the imperial power through the growing bureaucracy.

Geographically based on the Chinese agricultural region of Manchuria, the whole Manchu state tended thus more and more towards a bureaucratic Chinese form of organization. The conception of the state, developed simultaneously, showed the same trends. As the state grew in the margin of China, the ideas grew in the margin of Confucianism. The military virtues of the warriors, the pride of the feudal nobility of the frontier, the clan cohesion, remained for some time at least. But the thought turned more and more to China and to a Chinese kind of rulership over the

Chinese world. At the same time the policy towards the other frontier, the Mongol world, was similar to, though perhaps more efficient, than the Chinese colonial policy. The Manchus, having started at the Chinese frontier, were ready now to play their part in the affairs of China Proper.

* * *

The period of Manchu growth was a period of decline for the ruling Chinese dynasty, the Ming. Corruption and weakness at the court, famine and rebellion in the country showed that the Ming cycle was nearing its end. There was a chance for a new dynasty to establish itself, to end corruption, cut down the personal profits of the official class and reestablish order. The question was whether the new power would come from the border or from within China.

The only border power ready to move in was the Manchus, who saw their chance and who had worked and prepared for this time. But they had to compete with the Chinese bandit leader Li Tse-cheng,[1] who tried to establish a new dynasty from within. It is interesting enough to compare Li's background with the Manchu organization, for neither of the two competing powers had at the outset a decisive strategical advantage over the other. The decision in favor of the Manchus indicated rather that something in their organization and political conception must have been stronger than their rival's preparation for his attempt at the throne.[2]

Li, born in northern Shensi province, had started out as a robber and bandit and never forgot his past. In the twenties and thirties of the sixteenth century Li had been the leader of small and large bandit groups as they sprang up at the time in the famine stricken regions of northwestern China.

[1] See the life history of Li Tse-ch'eng in *Ming Shih*, Chapter 309, translation by E. Hauer in *Asia Major*, July-Oct., 1925.

[2] In the introduction to his translation of Li Tse-ch'engs biography Hauer declares that the horrors of civil war made the "tormented Chinese salute the Manchus as liberators" and thus made it possible "that a handful of half civilized Tungus could occupy by 'coup de main' the imperial throne of a giant empire." It is difficult to see how Hauer, who had at the same time completed the translation of the *K'ai Kuo Fang Lüeh* could interpret the Manchu conquest in this way, doing so little justice to the Manchu state.

With his bandits Li had raided unsystematically Shensi, Shansi, Honan, Hupeh, Szechuan, Kansu and even Anhui provinces. It was an up and down bandit fortune without any higher aims. Finally Li was cornered in South Shensi and brought near to suicide or surrender. But he considered the matter, ordered his group to kill all their family adherents and women, leave the baggage and move as a light cavalry force into Honan and Hupeh. There he found in 1639 in the basin of the Han river a new base of operations as famine brought him new followers and success. Sustained by this important region the former bandit developed political ambitions and conceived the idea of becoming emperor himself. Members of the scholar class, a " Dr." Niu and a " Dr." Li Chi became his advisers. The slaughtering technique was abandoned and a political organization undertaken.[3] Hsiangyang on the Han river became Li's first capital. Offices and designations of rank were created such as Prime Minister, Left and Right Chancellors, Presidents, Councillors and secretaries of six ministries, established according to Chinese tradition. Commanders were placed at strategic places and governors appointed over the districts controlled.[4]

From this base Li penetrated Shensi and Shansi[5] and broke through the pass of Nankou, attacking Peking. He

[3] Honanfu in the north, Ichang in the south had been conquered and added to the territory that was now to be politically organized.

[4] Many of the offices remained, however, pseudo appointments on paper only and the controlled districts were somewhat scattered.

[5] Before this move an important council had been held. Three routes of march came under discussion. One was to move through Honan straight up to the capital, Peking. It was the shortest and straightest way of attack but certainly the most exposed and unsafe one with only the small base in the Han valley as starting point. Two other possibilities offered themselves. One was to move down the Yangtse valley and first gain control of the rich economic area of the lower Yangtse to cut Peking off from its rice supplies and income from this key economic region. The third possibility was the strategic approach. The proposal was to move into Shensi and Shansi where probably connections from bandit times would help the conquest. This last way was chosen by Li. Strategically it was the best decision, but it indicated that strategic considerations led to the neglect of economic stability. Li did not seek this stability as he did not want to compromise with the ruling group.

conquered the city, drove the last Ming emperor to suicide and thus seemed to hold the palm of victory in his hand.

In the contest with the Manchus Li had thus the advantage of having reached the prize first. Whether he would be able to hold it would depend on his basic strength compared with that of the Manchus. Li's strategic position was rather strong, as he held, with the Han basin, Shansi, and the Tungkuan pass and the mountains of Shansi, all the military key positions to the control of North China, except the Manchurian border.

That Li finally failed was due to his weakness in the economic field and the fact that he did not really gain the support of the leading Chinese class, the scholar-gentry and its members in high political and military offices. Li remained a rebel, a hater of the ruling class, of the landlords and the gentry. Of course, he had very little time to gain political stability and to turn from a rebel into the guarantor of peace and order. Five years was all the time that Li used to organize his attempt at founding a dynasty, and the whole conquest of Shensi, Shansi and Peking happened in the last of these five years. Compared with the slow process of Manchu development, one must recognize the disadvantage of the inner Chinese rebel who had to march to quick victory. But even so he could have succeeded after he had gained control of the capital. What he needed was the support of people with decisive influence and administrative experience and in particular of the men in the decisive military positions. This support he could only gain if he turned from being a rebel to a protector in principle of the scholar-gentry class and the system of Chinese bureaucratic administration under it. But Li could not make in time his peace with the system in China. After his new start in Hsiangyang he followed for a time the advice of his scholar-councillors for a new constructive policy of trying to gain the support of all groups. But the bloodthirst of the bandit, looter and slaughterer he had been soon broke through again. Probably no Chinese rebellion was ever a soft affair, but the death and destruction Li left in his path—if one can believe his official biography [6]—was unusual, largely undid his military achievements and deprived him of the value of his own bases.

What was more important, Li's attitude cost him the sympathy of the group on whose support he depended and in particular of the man who held the strategic key position at the frontier. This man was the Chinese general Wu San-kwei, the commander of the troops at Shanhaikuan. He refused to go over to Li, and when Li marched against him, he called for the help of the Manchus and together with them defeated Li's armies. By doing so, however, he opened the gate of China to the Manchus, who took Peking and established their own dynasty there. Wu San-kwei had thus decided the struggle in favor of the Manchus. It was his act that gained the Manchus their first victory at Shanhaikuan.

The treason of Wu San-kwei to the Chinese cause has been dramatized in history. Much has been made of the touching story of his personal grief over the loss of his sweetheart who had been taken by a commander in the army of the bandit Li Tse-cheng.[7] But there was a deeper explanation. In contrast to Li, who persecuted the official class, the Manchus had in their organization made use of Chinese officials in leading positions. They had in no way disturbed the system of the official class, the position of the landlord and the gentry. On the Manchu side there was for Wu therefore a life and career in the traditional Chinese style, while he could await only with concern Li's future

---

[6] See note 1.

[7] The history narrates how this girl that had been promised to Wu San-kwei had been taken by one of the underlings of Li Tse-ch'eng. Wu therefore is supposed to have made common cause with the Manchus because of his outraged love, and finally he indeed regained the girl in battle. See Wu San-kwei's biography in *Erh Chen Ch'uan* (also translated by Hauer). Owen Lattimore has pointed out that behind this touching personal story was hidden the fact that Wu came from a family in Manchuria where his father before him had held high office, a more important fact than his personal motives. With regard to his personal motives it can also be said that Wu did indeed regain the girl through his choice of action (would there not have been also another way?) but also caused the death of his father who had been taken as hostage by Li Tse-ch'eng and was killed when Wu turned against Li.

political plans. Many Chinese officials before Wu had already found a profitable career on the Manchu side, especially such Chinese officials, who, as also Wu himself, came from the Chinese basin of Manchuria.

Wu was probably even some time before he actually went over to the Manchus not unfavorably inclined towards this new power in Manchuria. Thus he had remained inactive at Shanhaikuan, when the Manchus raided China through Jehol. When the decisive hour came, the choice was for him, as his letters to the Manchus indicate, really between order—as he understood it—and the protection of his interests, which he then could find only on the Manchu side, and disorder on the side of the rebel Li. He choose the Manchus.

This choice was a first indication of how Chinese the Manchus had become, if a Chinese official would prefer them to a Chinese rebel. In the sense of the traditional Chinese system of government, the Manchus were more Chinese than Li Tse-cheng. That became even more apparent after the first victory at Shanhaikuan and the opening of the road into China for the Manchus. The officials in North China, particularly in Shantung province, were quick to surrender. It may be remembered, as we stated before, that Shantung had been the province from which had come many of the families that had immigrated into Manchuria. And with the possession of Shantung the Manchus gained control of the imperial canal and with it the approach to the grain taxes of the Yangtse valley.

The Manchus attempted even to use the argument of their conservative loyalty to the Chinese system with the remnants of the Ming in South China.[8] Here, however, they found resistance, which was later broken by the force of arms.

Li Tse-cheng, on the other hand, could nowhere rally his forces again to an effective stand. He was chased from defeat to defeat all the way back to whence he had come, from Shansi to Shensi and, after a vain attempt to break into Sze-chuan, he was finally driven into the Han valley,

[8] See the argumentation in Hsieh Pao-chao, *op. cit.*, against the "legality" pretended in the exchange of letters with the Ming. See Chapter I, note 8.

from where he had started. His power simply collapsed and he withdrew into the Kiukiang mountains south of Wuchang. There he was killed by farmers into whose hands he fell on a foraging raid. Li's inability to draw any new strength from his bases after his first defeat, his collapse that came as quickly as his former rise to power, indicate the loose background of his whole adventure and the lack of support from regional sources that could command tax income and manpower.

The Manchus' newly gained power and rule, on the other hand, was " Chinese" enough to be acceptable to the Chinese. Thus, as a result of their largely Chinese organization and with the support of a majority of Chinese officials and soldiers, the Manchus occupied the throne in Peking as the new Ch'ing dynasty. It sounds very Confucian and Chinese, when one reads the Manchu proclamation that the " wheel of the world " had turned, the decline of one dynasty had made room for another, the Ming had lost the heavenly mandate. " Through heaven's favor and the new emperor's blessing" the Manchus had conquered Peking.[9]

Yet it was not the same as if the robber Li had become " fit for society " and had succeeded or as if another Chinese leader had established a new dynasty. The difference was discernible from the proclamation of the emperor which read: " Consequently one has elevated our old state to receive the new mandate." [10]

This sentence expressed the fact that the Manchus had marched into China not as a dynasty alone, nor as a simple barbarian horde, but as a state organization. The state which they had organized in Manchuria they now transferred into China. The state was not a " foreign nation " that conquered China. It was a partly foreign frontier organization which the Manchus brought. The banners, as has been said, had Manchu, Mongol and Chinese units. Even in the Manchu units only little more than half the people were of Manchu

[9] 天眷及皇上洪福巳克燕京 *Tung Hua Lu*, Shun Chih 2, p. 26.
[10] 逐舉舊邦誕膺新命 *K.K.F.L.*, end and *Tung Hua Lu*, Shun Chih, *ibid*.

or Juchen origin.[11] And intermarriage made it difficult to say how genuinely Manchu they were. But it was still a separate political organization, a state.

Would the Manchus, now in control of China, dissolve this organization or transform it by the inclusion of the whole Chinese government in its frame? They did neither. They " elevated the state to receive the new mandate."

The Manchus accepted the Chinese administration in China as they had formerly done in Manchuria.[12] They confirmed all surrendering officials in their posts, only introducing a stricter control with the threat that from then on no corruption would be tolerated. They emphasized, as they had frequently done in Manchuria, that they would not make any racial distinctions among their subjects. Chinese, Manchu and Mongol all were to be equally cared for.[13] But to organize all China in the same way as Manchuria was of course impossible. What suited the frontier did not suite the whole of China.

But the original organization was nevertheless still of importance. Any reorganization that would bring the whole of China into the Manchu state, or, rather, would dissolve the Manchu state into the government of China, would destroy the balance which the Manchus held in their frontier organization. It would also destroy the source of their power, aside from the fact that it would be a new difficulty to integrate the noble Manchus with the state.

Hence the Manchus kept their banner organization. The central government, established in their Manchurian capital, was also kept independent. Five of the six ministries in Mukden were maintained as branches of the new ministries

[11] Haenisch, op. cit., points out that of the banner families of that time only little more than half were of Manchu or Tungus origin. The handbook of the banner organization of 1735 counts 1,100 families, about 250 of whom were of Chinese, 200 of Mongol, 40 of Korean origin. All these had intermarried with the exception of the purely Manchu imperial house and a few noble families.

[12] Only in Southwest China did they nominate three great vassal princes, who were later abolished after a suppressed rebellion. The vassal princes were deserving Chinese partisans, one of them Wu San-kwei.

[13] 同屬朝廷志子. Tung Hua Lu, 3, p. 4.

of the central government in Peking, the ministry of the interior being the only exception.[14] Manchuria thus remained under the central control of Peking a frontier state and the basis of the Manchu banners and their power.

The banners had at first been the Manchu state. Now they became a state within the state. The frontier state was elevated and its people became a sort of hereditary privileged group. Units of the banners were strategically distributed over the country and their commanders ranked higher than the officials of the administration without having themselves administrative functions other than those connected with the life of their subordinate banner people.[15] The function of the banners had thus changed. They became a centralizing and controlling factor, strategically located as they were over the provinces and around and in the capital. This distribution was perhaps the most important factor in the greater and stricter centralization which the new dynasty brought at the outset.[16]

In this survival of the frontier state in partly new form, could be seen also the main difference between a Chinese dynasty originating from an inner rebellion in China and a dynasty that had organized its power on the frontier. In this regard the frontier power was different from the rebellious Chinese force. It has been stated before that in contrast to the rebellion which either won or failed and did not know any intermediary status, the frontier had its own *raison d'etre* regardless of whether it succeeded in gaining or even attempted to gain the throne. If it did succeed, however, it could not entirely denounce its own *raison*, even after taking over the throne of all China.

This difference was felt on both sides. The privileges of the banner people, of whom so many were Chinese them-

[14] These branch ministries in Mukden were abolished only in 1907.

[15] The comparison with party troops in totalitarian states is tempting.

[16] Many other reforms indicate this centralization, for instance the excellent system of postal communication which the Board of War organized. Post stations had existed under the Ming, but their functioning had greatly deteriorated like many other government functions. A censor could even propose their abolishment for economies sake! (Hauer, *Li Tse-ch'eng*, p. 444.)

selves, irked the Chinese people more than those of the " alien race" of the Manchus.[17] The un-Chinese part of the organization seemed "barbarian" to the Chinese and indicated the frontier origin.

Against this reproach the Manchus set their noble descent. Already Nuerhaci had indicated that the Manchus as proud seigneurs and vassals were of higher standing than the ancestor of the Ming dynasty who had been a monk.[18] In the introduction of the *K'ai Kuo Fang Lueh* the famous emperor Ch'ien Lung took up the same idea. He stated that none of the racially Chinese dynasties could have the authority of the Mongol or Manchu dynasties, for all the others had come from the common people of China. Mongols and Manchus had been noble vassals. In his heart the Manchu felt superior to the Chinese, felt something of the pride of his feudal military past.

The Manchus never became completely absorbed into the Chinese culture. They remained the privileged group of conquerors; the group which retained part of the military and feudal past all through its history. A Manchu would always have his bowl of rice, a small pension at least, paid to the member of the conquering group by the conquered people. The Manchu warriors still practiced archery when the modern guns and gunboats of he West had already forced another civilization on China.

On the throne in Peking the Manchus thus remained tied to their past history. And in this history the frontier had interacted with the Chinese tradition. In their Chinese bureaucratic organization the Manchus never quite lost the frontier touch. But the frontier, with its own characteristics, formed also a part of the general scenery of China's political history. The great idea of Chinese civilization embraced also the frontier development. Even the Manchu superiority could not conceal the fact that it was the Chinese civilization which had to be recognized as their political and ideological standard by the Manchus too.

[17] Haenisch, *op. cit.*
[18] *K. K. F. L.,* Chapter XXII, p. 16.

ANNEX

LI YUNG-FANG. *Erh Chen Ch'uan*, book 1, pages 42-49.

Li Yung-fang was a native of Tiehling in Liaotung. In the 41st year Wan Li of the Ming (1613) he defended Fushun with the rank of major. At that time the Yehe Beile Gintaisi and Buyanggu sent a Mongol to the Ming and informed them as follows: " The three states of the Hata, Hoifa and Ula have been already completely conquered by the Manchus. If they attack us now again, their intention is to attack forthwith the Ming." The Ming ordered the major to strengthen at once the troops of the mountain passes, and to prepare 1000 men with fireweapons in order to defend the two Fang and Hsi-towns of the Yehe. Then they sent a messenger to our ruler and said one should not attack, but reestablish friendly relations and dismiss the troops.

When T'ai-tsu had received the letter, he wrote the Ming: " In the past the Yehe, Hata, Ula and Hoifa, the Korcin and Sibe, Guwalca, Juseri and Neyen, the countries of nine tribes have in the year Kwei-si (1593) assembled their troops in order to attack us. We collected troops for defense and heaven disapproved of injustice. Our troops had a great victory, beheaded the Yehe Beile Bujai and captured the Ula Beile Bujantai, who was sent back again into his country. Then in the year Tingyu (1597) a horse was slaughtered and an alliance sworn over the blood. One became connected by marriage and was not to forget the good relationship. Who would have thought that the Yehe would disavow the old alliance? They regretted that they had promised the girl and did not give her away. With regard to Bujantai, I have treated him with favour. He has paid for decency with hatred. Therefore I have punished him, annihilated his army and taken his country. Now Bujantai has fled to the Yehe. The Yehe have received him and did not hand him over to me. Therefore I now chastise the Yehe. With regard to the Ming, what mistrust or hatred should arouse in me the wish that we attack each other? "

After he had conceived the letter he went with his followers to Fushun; at this Li Yung-fang went three miles out of the town to welcome him. He led him to the training ground. After T'ai-tsung had handed over the letter, he returned.

120

Not long after the Ming general Chang Ch'eng-yin placed
signposts and made it known that the districts Ch'ai-ho, Sanch'a
and Fu-an, situated within the borders of our soldier settlements,
could not be harvested. The governor Li Wei-han furthermore kept
our envoys Kangguri, Fanggina and others, in order to revenge
the people captured and killed for passing over the frontier. In the
4th month of the third year Tien Ming of our dynasty, that is the
46th year Wan Li of the Ming (May 1618), T'ai-tsu announced
to heaven the seven great complaints. Then he brought up the army
to fight the Ming.

To Li Yung-fang he communicated in a letter the following
order: " You have sent troops over the frontier and helped the
Yehe with protection. Thus I have called up the army and am
coming. You are in Fushun only a major. Even if you fight, you
will certainly not win. Now I order you to capitulate. If you surrender, my troops will penetrate to-day deep into the country. If you
do not surrender you delay the time of our invasion. You have
always been an intelligent man with a sound grasp of present requirements. Our state has always had a generous understanding of
talented men. And if one is somewhat gifted and quick in
administration, one elevates him, appoints him and binds him by
marriage. And all the more with a man like you one must show
special esteem and place him in the same rank with our first dignitaries. If you do not fight, but surrender, I shall let you keep
your former office and shall care benevolently for you. But if you
fight, how can our arrows know who you are? You will find death
in the shower of arrows. If one has no chance to win victory, of
what use then is death? Besides, if you come out of the town and
surrender, our troops shall not penetrate into the town and your
officers and men will all remain unharmed. But if our soldiers
invade the town, old and young, men and women, will face terror
and ruin; that will also be of no advantage to you. Do not say
that we make empty threats that must not be believed. Think. If I
could not take such a small town, what purpose would it serve to call
up the army? If you miss your chance and do not make up your mind,
regret will also be of no avail. If the high and low officers, and
soldiers and the people in the town surrender the town and submit,
then their parents, wives and children and all the families shall be
protected and also not be separated. Is that not wonderful? To
surrender or not, think it over well, and disobey not my words in the

indignation of the passing hour, so that anger should destroy this possibility and a chance be missed."

Yung-fang received the ruler's letter. He knew that a great army had come. In his official attire he stood at the south gate of the town but ordered his troops to prepare all for defense. In a moment our troops put up the scaling ladders and climbed on to the wall. The defenders were thrown into disorder and terror. Then Yung-fang mounted his horse and came out and surrendered. When our banner dignitary Adun led him before the emperor, he threw himself down and remained long on the ground to accept his fate.

The people in the town surrendered as did the two towns Tung-chou and Mahatan and also over 500 castles and posts. Whoever prepared defense and did not surrender in spite of the ruler's order was killed.

Chang Ch'eng-yin from Kuangning with lieutenant-general P'o Feng-hsiang from Liaoyang, the lieutenant-colonel P'u Shih-fang from Haichow, the major Liang Ju-kuei and others came to help with over 10,000 troops; they all were killed in battle.

The ruler ordered Fushun to be destroyed and the conquered people of 1000 families to be grouped and settled in Hsinking. As formerly under the Ming, high and low officials were appointed. They were placed under Yung-fang, who was made deputy general and appointed to govern the subjected people. He was married to a daughter of the Beile Abatai, the seventh son of the ruler.

In the seventh month of this year (1618) he took part in the campaign of the ruler against the Ming. Lieutenant-general Tsou Ch'u-hsien of Tsingho was asked to surrender. Ch'u-hsien did not obey. Together with the lieutenant-colonel Chang Pe he was killed in battle at the head of 10,000 men. The town was then conquered.

In the 4th year (1619) the ruler went with the whole army against the Ming town T'iehling. In the 6th year (1621) Mukden and Liaoyang were taken. Yung-fang took part in these campaigns, earned merits and was promoted to the grade of general. The Ming governor Wang Hua-cheng and the frontier generals continuously sent messengers to entice Yung-fang away. He arrested these people with the letters and informed the ruler. He was commended and granted pardon from capital punishment three times in advance by imperial command.

In the first year T'ien Tsung (1627) the Ming general Mao Wen-
lung was established on the islands off the shore of Korea. The
Beiles Amin and Jirgalang and others, the high officials Yang-
guri and Namtai together with Yung-fang were ordered to lead
the troops against Korea. The emperor ordered them to ask Korea
in a proper way to submit, not to take everything, but to act according to occasion and with fairness. Then they conquered at first Jehou
in Korea. They sent troops that attacked T'ieshan and drove Mao
Wen-lung away. Then Tingchow in Korea was stormed. In Tingchow they took prisoners and killed a great number of people.
Then the army reached the town of Ping-yang. The officials and the
people had all run away. The Tatungkiang was crossed. The king
of Korea sent envoys with a letter to meet them. The Beile received
the letter, in which several times excuse for former disrespect was
offered. They granted that he should send a trusted high official
to apologize and conclude an alliance; then they would lead the
army back. The army reached Huangchow. Li-tsung sent a mounted
messenger with the information that trusted high officials were already
on the way to swear an alliance. But the Beile Amin wanted nevertheless to attack. Yung-fang said to all the Beiles: "We have received the
highest command to be fair. In the recent exchange of letters with
Korea we said that we would lead the troops back if a trusted high
dignitary should come, apologize and swear an alliance. If we now
break our former word, it is unjust. One should rather remain here
for a while and wait." All the Beiles agreed with his words. Only
Amin shouted furiously at Yung-fang and said: "You Chinese
slave. Why all these words? I should kill you." Then they marched
on Pingshan. Li-tsung thereupon sent trusted high dignitaries and his
younger brother the Yuan-ch'ang-chün Li Chüeh. After their arrival
Amin said to all the Beiles. I have always had a desire to see the capital and the palace of the Ming emperor and of the king of Korea
but have never seen them. As we are now so near the capital of Korea,
how can we turn back without going there. We must move to their
hole and then see further. The Beile Yoto, Jirgalang, Ajige and
Dudu were all of the opinion that one could not do this. At last,
as Yung-fang had formerly advised, they sent the lieutenant-general
Liu Hsing-tsu and others to conclude the alliance and turned back.

In the 5th month of the 8th year (1634) all officials were rewarded for their performances. At that time Yung-fang, who had

received at the time of his surrender the rank of a Viscount of the third class, received his rank as hereditary without discontinuation. In the same year he died. He had nine sons, who served in the blue Chinese banner. All received official appointments. The second son had the rank of a high official. He became state secretary and governor-general. The third son, Kang A, was a high official and moved up to the position of a general. The fifth son Kang Yen was hereditary Viscount and became lieutenant-general. All had descendants.

BIBLIOGRAPHY

(Note: No claim is made to give an exhaustive bibliography of the subject. The books and articles named are only those mentioned and quoted in the text.)

CHINESE HISTORICAL TEXTS:

K'ai Ming. Erh Shih Wu Shih, Ming Shih. (開明. 二十五史, 明史).
The K'ai Ming edition, Shanghai, of the "twenty-five Dynastic Histories," Ming History.

Huang-Ch'ing K'ai-Kuo Fang-lueh. (皇清開國方略.)
History of the foundation of the Manchu Empire. Imperial ed. with Emperor Ch'ien Lung's facsimile introduction of 1786, quoted *K. K. F. L.*

Shih-Ch'ao Tung Hua Lu. (十朝東華錄.)
History of the period of government of 10 emperors of the Manchu dynasty. 1583-1861.

Ta Ch'ing Hui Tien. (大清會典.)
"Institutions" of the Manchu Empire. Peping, 1818 ed.

Pa-Ch'i T'ung-Chih. (八旗通志.)
Description of the eight banners, fourth year Ch'ien-Lung.

Pa-ch'i Man-chow Shih-tsu T'ung-p'u (八旗滿洲氏族通譜). Comprehensive genealogy of the Manchu clans, 1745.

Wei Yüan, Sheng Wu Chi. (聖武紀.)
History of the Wars of the Manchu Emperors.

Man-Han, Ming Chen Ch'uan. (滿漢明臣傳.)
Biographies of famous Manchu and Chinese officials under the Manchu dynasty.

Erh Chen Ch'uan. (貳臣傳)
Biographies of officials who served under two dynasties (the Ming and the Manchu).

TRANSLATIONS

Huang-Ts'ing K'ai-Kuo Fang-Lüeh, Die Gründung des Mandschurischen Kaiserreiches, übersetzt und erklärt von Erich Hauer, Berlin und Leipzig, 1926.

"Li T'ze-ch'eng und Chang Hsien-chung, ein Beitrag zum Ende der Ming Dynastie," translated from *Ming Shih,* Chapter 309, by Erich Hauer, *Asia Major,* Leipzig, July-Oct., 1925, April, 1926.

"Prinz Dorgon," translated from Ch'in Ting Tsung Shih Wang Kung Kung Chi Piao Ch'uan, by Erich Hauer, *Ostasiatische Zeitschrift,* Hamburg, *Neue Folge,* III, Heft 1, p. 9.

"General Wu San-kuei," translated from Erh Chen Ch'uan by Erich Hauer, *Asia Major,* Leipzig, Oct. 1927.

"Beiträge der frühen Geschichte der Manchu-dynastie. 1) Prinz Daisan,

2) die Prinzen Anim und Manggultai, 3) Prinz Jirgalang," translated from Ch'in Ting Tsung Shih Wang Kung Kung Chi Piao
Ch'uan by Erich Hauer, *Ostasiatische Zeitschrift,* Hamburg, 1926.

Обстоятельное описание происхождения и состояния маньджурскаго народа и войска в осми знаменах состоящаго, organization
of the Manchu banners, translated from Chinese ed. of 1739, St. Petersburg, 1784, in 12 volumes.

Geschichte der Grossen Liao aus dem Manchu übersetzt. Liao History,
translated by H. C. von der Gabelentz, St. Petersburg, 1877.

BOOKS AND ARTICLES

Chi Ch'ao-ting, *Key Economic Areas in Chinese History.* London, 1936.

Otto Franke, "Zur Beurteilung des chinesischen Lehenswesens," *Sitzungs-
bericht phil. hist. Kl. 1927,* Berlin, 1928.

Lucien Gibert, *Dictionnaire Historique et Géographique de la Manchourie,*
Hongkong, 1934.

W. Gorski, "Ueber die Herkunft des Stammvaters der jetzt in China herrschenden Dynastic Zin und vom Ursprung des Namens der Man-
tschsu." *Arbeiten der kais. russ. Gesandtschaft zu Peking über China,*
Berlin, 1858, 1st Vol., p. 347.

Marcel Granet, *La Civilisation Chinoise,* Paris, 1927.

E. Haenisch, "Die gegenwärtigen chinesischen Wirren und ihre geschichtlichen Voraussetzungen. *Vergangenheit und Gegenwart,* Vol. 18º,
65-82.

E. Haenisch, "Hosoi Cin Wang," *Asia Major,* Leipzig, II, 590.

Hsieh Pao-chao, *The Government of China.* (1644-1911), Baltimore, 1925.

Hsiu I-shan, *Ch'ing-tai t'ung-shih.* (清代通史.)
History of the Manchu Dynasty, 2 Vols, Shanghai, 1932.

A. W. Hummel, *Eminent Chinese of the Ch'ing Period,* biographical dictionary, in preparation.

Olga Lang, "The good Iron of the New Chinese Army," *Pacific Affairs,*
XII, New York, March, 1939.

Owen Lattimore, *Inner Asian Frontiers of China,* New York, 1940.

————, *The Gold Tribe, "Fishskin Tatars" of the lower Sungari.* Memoirs
Amer. Anthropological Soc., No. 40, 1933.

T. C. Lin, "Manchuria in the Ming Empire," *Nankai Social and Economic
Quarterly,* Tientsin, Vol. VIII, No. 1, 1935.

————, "Manchurian Trade and Tribute in the Ming Dynasty," *Nankai
Social and Economic Quarterly,* Tientsin, Vol. IX, No. 4, 1937.

J. Marquardt, *Die Chronologie der alttürkischen Inschriften,* Leipzig, 1898.

Willian Frederik Mayers, *The Chinese Government,* 3rd ed., Shanghai,
1896.

Meng Sen, *Ch'ing-Ch'ao Ch'ien-Chi* (孟森, 清朝前紀). A study of the
ancestry of the Ch'ing Dynasty, Shanghai, 1930.

Friedrich Otte, "Early Manchu Economy," *Chinese Economic Journal,* 1927.

S. M. Shirokogorov, *Social Organization of the Manchus,* Shanghai, 1924.

Arnold J. Toynbee, *A Study of History,* 6 Vols., London, 1934-39.

Wang Yü-chüan, "The Rise of Land Tax and the Fall of Dynasties in
Chinese History," *Pacific Affairs,* IX, New York, June, 1936.

Léon Wieger, *Textes Historiques, Histoire Politique de la Chine depuis l'origine, jusqu'en 1912,* 2 Vols., Hien-hien, 1922.

Henry R. Williamson, *Wang An Shih, A Chinese Statesman and Educationalist of the Sung Dynasty,* 2 Vols., London, 1935-37.

Karl August Wittfogel, *Probleme der chinesischen Wirtschaftsgeschichte,* Archiv für Sozialwissenschaft und Sozialpolitik, Tübingen, 1927.

————, " The Foundations and Stages of Chinese Economic History," *Zeitschrift für Sozialforschung,* IV, Heft 1, Paris, 1935.

————, " Die Theorie der Orientalischen Gesellschaft," *Zeitschrift für Sozialforschung,* VII, Doppelheft 1/2, Paris, 1938.

———— and Feng Chia-sheng, *History of Chinese Society,* Volume *Liao,* to appear soon.

————, *Oriental Society in Asia and Ancient America,* to appear soon.

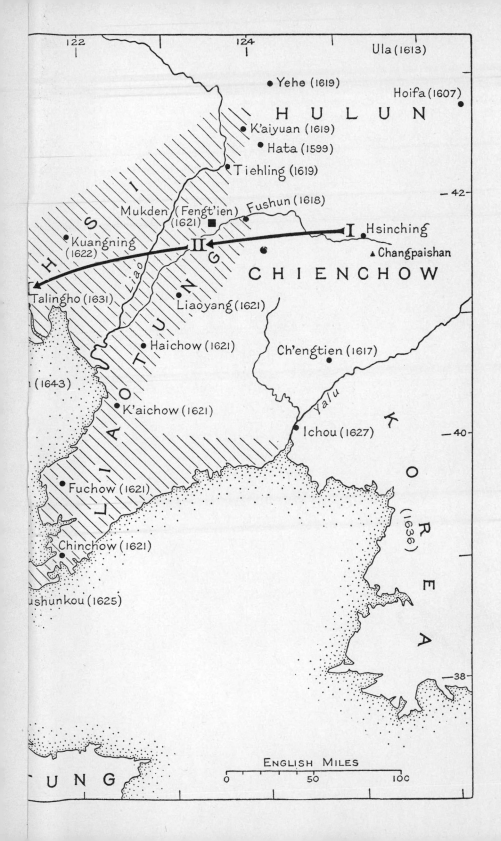

122

124

Ula (1613)

Yehe (1619)

Hoifa (1607)

H U L U N

K'aiyuan (1619)

Hata (1599)

Tiehling (1619)

42

Mukden (Fengt'ien)   Fushun (1618)

(1621) ■

I Hsinching

Kuangning
(1622)

II

Changpaishan

Talingho (1631)

Liao

C H I E N C H O W

Liaoyang (1621)

H S I   L I A O T U N G

Haichow (1621)

Ch'engtien (1617)

(1643)

Yalu

K

K'aichow (1621)

Ichou (1627)

40

O

Fuchow (1621)

R

(1636)

E

Chinchow (1621)

A

ushunkou (1625)

38

U N G

ENGLISH MILES

0   50   100